Children's Dishes

Children's Dishes

By
Margaret and Kenn Whitmyer

COLLECTOR BOOKS
P.O. Box 3009
Paducah, KY 42001

The current values in this book should be used only as a guide. They are not intended to set prices, which vary from one section of the country to another. Auction prices as well as dealer prices vary greatly and are affected by condition as well as demand. Neither the Author nor the Publisher assumes responsibility for any losses that might be incurred as a result of consulting this guide.

Additional copies of this book may be ordered from:

COLLECTOR BOOKS
P.O. Box 3009
Paducah, Kentucky 42001

@ $9.95 Add $1.00 for postage and handling.

Printed by IMAGE GRAPHICS, Paducah, Kentucky

Dedication

This book is dedicated to our sons, Quentin and Bryan, who persevered through this project.

Contents

7

Acknowledgements

We would like to take this opportunity to express our appreciation to the many people who helped make this book possible. Enthusiastic collectors and dealers from all over the country shared their collections, welcomed us into their homes, and spent many hours discussing their collections.

We would especially like to acknowledge the fine work of Mary Lou Esterline. Her vast knowledge of pattern glass and china proved invaluable and saved us many hours of exhausting research. We deeply appreciate all her time and effort.

We also greatly appreciate the hospitality extended to us by Parke and Joyce Bloyer, Jim and Nancy Maben, and George and Roni Sionakides. They invited us into their homes, and spent many hours packing glass, which enabled us to photograph their extensive collections. Also, they contributed many ideas and necessary pricing and historical information.

We also extend thanks to the many antique dealers who contacted us with interesting items. They have helped to make this book more complete. Their efforts were remarkable and are deeply appreciated.

We are also very grateful to the following people who loaned us parts of their collections or supplied us with valuable information: Ann Barnes, Miles Bausch, Fred Bickenheuser, Jim and Marietta Dalessandro, John and Rita Ebner, Don and Linda Fagley, Gene and Cathy Florence, Justine Geiser, Bill Heacock, William Horton, Joyce Johnson, Jack and Dorothy Jordan, Scott and Mary Kuder, Nora Koch, Jim Lamereoux, Merle and Dee Long, Bill and Minerva Lesher, Douglas Lucas, Gene and Mary Jo Massie, Ray and Nadine Pankow, Gerry Pugh, Marilyn Ross, Dick and Verylene Summers, Rick Teets, Bunny Walker, Katie Wilcox, Delmer and Mary Lou Youngen.

The efforts of our great photographer, Siegfried Kurz, are greatly appreciated. He had the patience and persistence to do a fine job under the most trying circumstances. We would also like to thank his wife, Pat, for allowing us to keep him working all those late nights.

Foreword

The purpose of this book is to give the collector a general idea of what is available, and at what prices children's dishes might be obtained. Included are sections on glass, china, metal, stoneware and plastic. An attempt has been made to identify the manufacturer, when possible. We have also tried to indicate pieces which have been reproduced.

Although as many sets as possible have been included in each area, there is no possible way we can say this book is complete. New discoveries are being made every day, and we hope we will be able to share some of them with you in the future.

Pricing

The prices in this book represent retail prices for mint condition pieces. A price range has been included to allow for some regional differences in price. This book is intended to be only a guide, and is not intended to set or establish prices.

Most sets have been priced both as sets and again with prices for each piece in the set. The prices listed are prices we have seen collectors pay, and also, those prices collectors have told us they would be willing to pay.

Reproductions

Compared to the number of items available in children's dishes, reproductions have not been a widespread problem. All pieces that we know have been reproduced will be noted, and the new colors will be indicated in a footnote.

Measurements

All measurements have been taken as follows to the nearest 1/16 inch:
Bowl - Diameter
Butter - Height to top of lid
Cakestand - Height
Casserole - Total length to handles
Creamer - Height to highest point
Cup - Height
Pitcher - Height to highest point
Plate - Diameter
Platter - Length
Saucer - Diameter
Spooner - Height
Sugar, open - Height
Sugar and lid - Height with lid
Teapot and lid - Height to top of lid
Tray - Diameter
Waste bowl - Height

PART I: GLASS

Akro Agate Company

The Akro Agate Company was established in Akron, Ohio, in 1911. In 1914, the company moved to Clarksburg, West Virginia, where it remained until it closed its doors in 1951. Akro Agate was a major producer of marbles and games. Doll dishes were introduced in the 1930's, but didn't sell well until World War II restricted Japanese imports. Most of the pieces bear the Akro Agate trademark-- a crow flying through the letter "A".

J. Pressman (Akro Agate Co.)
"Tea for Six"

These cups and saucers exist in a variety of colors and were also sold as demitasse sets. All the children's sets we have found have contained the opaque green cups and saucers. Due to the crudeness and the lackluster appearance of the cups and saucers, most collectors want this set in the original box.

Tea for Six	Opaque Green
Cup	3.50- 4.00
Saucer	1.50- 2.00
Boxed Set, 12 piece	37.50-40.00

J. Pressman (Akro Agate Co.)
"Pastry Set"

This is another set with Chiquita-like pieces. The set consists of two glass cake pans, a glass covered bowl, a wooden rolling pin, a wooden mixer, metal cookie cutters, and a recipe book. The small baker is frequently found since it was also used in a "Tiddly Wink" set. Since the metal pieces are also commonly found, a boxed set is more desirable to collectors.

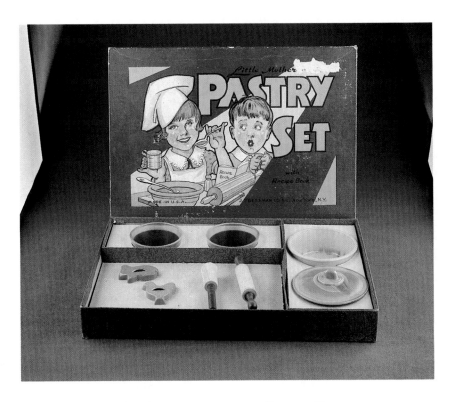

Pastry Set	Opaque Green
Cake Pan	7.00- 8.00
Casserole, covered	24.00-26.00
Set in Box, 9 piece	45.00-55.00

J.P. (Akro Agate Co.)

These large-size toy dishes were made for the J. Pressman Company. The baked-on sets include cereal bowls, which are not present in the smaller "Chiquita" sets. "J.P." is found in transparent green, transparent blue, transparent brown, and baked-on colors. A few sets have been seen in transparent deep red. Some pieces of the blue-tinted crystal have also been found. Although there is a demand for the transparent colored pieces, the baked on items are not very appealing to most collectors.

The cobalt set with vertical ribs, on the left, is a J.P.-type set, although no proof has surfaced that this is actually an Akro Agate product. Maybe someone will turn up a boxed set which will identify the maker.

J.P.	Transparent Green/ Cobalt*	Transparent Red/Brown	Baked-On Colors	Trans Cobalt With Ribs
Cereal, 3-13/16″	-------	-------	5.00- 6.00	-------
Creamer, 1½″	20.00- 22.50	25.00- 27.50	5.00- 6.50	-------
Cup, 1½″	11.00- 13.00	15.00- 18.00	3.50- 4.00	3.50- 4.00
Plate, 4¼″	7.50- 8.50	10.00- 12.50	1.50- 2.00	3.50- 4.00
Saucer, 3¼″	3.50- 4.00	6.00- 7.50	1.25- 1.50	2.00- 2.50
Sugar and Lid, 1½″	22.50- 25.00	30.00- 32.50	6.00- 7.50	-------
Teapot and Lid, 1½″	25.00- 27.50	37.50- 40.00	12.00-13.50	-------
Boxed Set, 17 pieces	160.00-182.00	221.00-258.00	53.00-63.00	-------
Boxed Set, 21 pieces			73.00-89.00	

* Crystal 50% higher

Chiquita (Akro Agate Co.)

"Chiquita" sets were made for the J. Pressman Company of New York. Pieces which are marked have "J.P." embossed on the bottom.

The most commonly found color is green opaque. Transparent cobalt is found frequently, but the opaque colors, which include light blue, turquoise, lavender, caramel, and yellow, are elusive. Some blue-tinted pieces, such as the teapot on the right of the photo have surfaced. Also on the right in the photo is a boxed set of baked-on colors. The boxed set on the left included a tablecloth and napkins which could be embroidered.

The crude shape and poor quality of these pieces are responsible for the low demand among Akro collectors. Except for a few items in the harder to find colors, prices have remained low.

Chiquita	Green Opaque	Other Opaques	Trans Cobalt*	Baked on Colors
Creamer, 1½ "	3.75- 4.25	7.00- 7.50	8.50- 9.00	5.00- 5.50
Cup, 1½ "	3.00- 4.00	7.50- 8.00	4.50- 5.00	4.00- 4.50
Plate, 3¾ "	1.75- 2.25	-------	5.00- 5.50	1.50- 1.75
Saucer, 3 1/8 "	1.50- 2.00	2.00- 2.50	2.50- 3.00	1.00- 1.25
Sugar, no Lid, 1½ "	3.50- 4.00	6.00- 7.00	6.50- 7.50	4.00- 4.50
Teapot and Lid, 3 "	8.50- 9.00	14.00-16.00	15.00- 17.00	12.00-13.00
Boxed Set, 16 Piece	45.00-55.00	77.00-85.00	107.00-120.00	56.00-58.00
Boxed Set, 22 piece	60.00-72.50			

Tablecloth and 4 napkins, $25.00 set.
*Crystal 50% higher

Concentric Rib (Akro Agate Co.)

"Concentric Rib" and "Concentric Ring" are often confused. Cups, saucers and plates in both sets contain a series of narrowly spaced rings. However, "Concentric Rib" sets are of poor quality and always contain "Stacked Disc" teapots, sugars, and creamers. Many sets are found containing opaque green and white pieces. Other colors include opaque pink, and opaque blue, with the teapot, sugar and creamer appearing in the full range of "Stacked Disc" colors.

Concentric Rib	Green/White	Other Opaque Colors
Creamer, 1¼"	3.50- 4.50	4.00- 5.50
Cup, 1¼"	2.00- 2.50	2.50- 3.50
Plate, 3¼"	1.50- 2.00	2.50- 3.00
Saucer, 2¾"	1.50- 2.00	1.50- 2.50
Sugar, 1¼"	3.50- 4.50	4.00- 5.50
Teapot and Lid, 3-3/8"	6.00- 7.00	7.50- 8.50
Set in Box, 7 piece	21.00-25.00	25.00-30.00

Concentric Ring, Large and Small (Akro Agate Co.)

Large "Concentric Ring" sets come in a variety of color combinations. Although they are elusive, the most desirable colors are transparent cobalt, opaque pumpkin, and lavender. "Concentric Ring" cups, saucers, plates, and cereal bowls are distinguished by a series of narrow, closely spaced, horizontal raised rings. The sugar, creamer, teapot, and lids are the same as "Stacked Disc and Interior Panel". In the photo on page 16 the boxed set and the lavender cup are large size. The lavender cup in the foreground is quite unusual because the rings continue all the way to the base, instead of being confined to a narrow band around the center. The cup also has interior panels as is shown in the photo below.

Large Size	Transparent Cobalt	Blue Marbleized	Other Opaque Colors
Cereal, 3-3/8 "	22.00- 25.00	27.50- 30.00	15.00- 17.00
Creamer, 1-3/8 "	22.00- 25.00	30.00- 35.00	10.00- 12.00
*Cup, 1-3/8 "	22.00- 25.00	25.00- 30.00	12.00- 14.00
Plate, 4¼ "	10.00- 12.00	15.00- 17.00	6.00- 7.00
Saucer, 3-1/8 "	5.00- 7.50	8.00- 9.00	4.00- 5.00
Sugar and Lid, 1-7/8 "	30.00- 32.50	35.00- 40.00	16.00- 18.00
Teapot and Lid, 3¾ "	35.00- 40.00	45.00- 50.00	30.00- 35.00
Boxed Set, 21 piece	325.00-375.00	420.00-460.00	210.00-235.00

*Pumpkin $14.00; yellow $15.00; lavender $22.00

Small Size	Transparent Cobalt	Blue Marbleized	Other Opaque Colors
Creamer, 1¼"	18.00- 20.00	24.00- 26.00	8.00- 10.00
Cup, 1¼"	24.00- 26.00	27.00- 29.00	8.00- 10.00
Plate, 3¼"	10.00- 12.00	11.00- 13.00	4.00- 6.00
Saucer, 2¾"	7.50- 9.50	8.00- 10.00	2.50- 3.50
Sugar, 1¼"	18.00- 20.00	24.00- 26.00	8.00- 10.00
Teapot and Lid, 3-3/8"	27.00- 30.00	50.00- 55.00	12.00- 14.00
Boxed Set, 16 Piece	230.00-260.00	290.00-320.00	90.00-115.00

Concentric Ring, Large and Small

Interior Panel, Small (Akro Agate Co.)

"Interior Panel" pieces have panels on the top of the plates, and inside of cups, sugars, creamers, teapots, lids, pitchers and tumblers. The pitcher and tumblers are commonly found in transparent green and amber. A few opaque tumblers have been seen. There are two styles of green pitchers and tumblers. In one style the verticle panels continue to the top edge. In the other there is a horizontal band around the top edge which lacks panels. Some pieces also have a stippled effect (see "Stippled Band", small) and have become known as "Stippled Interior Panel".

Interior Panel, Small	Pink/Green Luster		Azure Blue Yellow		Transparent Green/Topaz	
Creamer, 1¼"	20.00-	22.00	24.00-	27.00‡‡	8.00-	10.00
Cup, 1¼"	6.50-	8.00	22.00-	25.00*	5.50-	6.50
Pitcher, 2-7/8"	-------		-------		8.00-	9.00
Plate, 3¾"	3.50-	4.00	4.00-	6.00	2.50-	3.50
Saucer, 2-3/8"	2.50-	3.00	5.00-	7.00	3.00-	3.50
Sugar, 1¼"	20.00-	22.00	24.00-	27.00‡‡	8.00-	10.00
Teapot and Lid, 3-3/8"	12.00-	15.00	30.00-	32.00†	9.00-	10.00
Tumbler, 2"	20.00-	25.00	-------		5.50-	6.50
Boxed Set, 8 piece	35.00-	45.00	95.00-	110.00	30.00-	40.00
Boxed Set, 16 piece	105.00-	120.00	210.00-	235.00	75.00-	90.00

*Pumpkin 50% less; †Cobalt 50% less; ‡‡Cobalt $8.00-10.00.

Interior Panel, Small	Blue & White Marbleized		Red & White Marbleized		Green & White Marbleized	
Creamer, 1¼"	20.00-	22.00	22.00-	25.00	13.00-	15.00
Cup, 1¼"	18.00-	20.00	20.00-	22.00	9.00-	10.00
Pitcher, 2-7/8"	-------		-------		-------	
Plate, 3¾"	8.50	9.50	6.00-	7.00	5.00-	6.00
Saucer, 2-3/8"	6.00-	7.00	6.00-	7.00	3.50-	4.50
Sugar, 1¼"	20.00-	22.00	22.00-	25.00	14.00-	15.00
Teapot and Lid, 3-3/8"	30.00-	32.00	18.00-	20.00	19.00-	21.00
Tumbler, 2"	-------		-------		-------	
Boxed Set, 8 piece	100.00-	110.00	85.00-	95.00	55.00-	65.00
Boxed Set, 16 piece	210.00-	225.00	195.00-	220.00	115.00-	130.00

Interior Panel, Large (Akro Agate Co.)

"Interior Panel" pieces have panels on the top of the plates, and inside of bowls, cups, sugars, creamers, teapots, and lids. "Interior panel" differs from "Stacked Disc and Interior Panel" since all "Interior Panel" pieces are smooth on the underside of plates and on the exterior of other pieces.

Beware of buying individual pieces of topaz, since there are two different shades. All "Interior Panel" colors are highly collectible, although the marbleized colors rate slightly higher.

Interior Panel, Large	Blue & White Marbleized	Red & White Marbleized	Green & White Marbleized
Cereal, 3-3/8"	20.00- 22.00	22.50- 25.00	16.00- 18.00
Creamer, 1-3/8"	20.00- 22.00	22.50- 25.00	16.00- 18.00
Cup, 1-3/8"	18.00- 20.00	19.00- 21.00	13.00- 15.00
Plate, 4¼"	8.00- 10.00	8.00- 10.00	7.00- 9.00
Saucer, 3-1/8"	6.00- 7.00	7.00- 8.00	6.00- 7.00
Sugar and Lid, 1-7/8"	27.00- 30.00	29.00- 31.00	20.00- 22.00
Teapot and Lid, 3¾"	35.00- 37.00	37.50- 42.00	28.00- 32.00
Boxed Set, 21 piece	295.00-325.00	320.00-350.00	237.00-265.00

Interior Panel, Large	Lemonade & Oxblood	Transparent Green	Transparent Topaz
Cereal, 3-3/8"	22.00- 25.00	9.00- 11.00	8.00- 10.00
Creamer, 1-3/8"	22.00- 25.00	9.00- 11.00	8.00- 9.00
Cup, 1-3/8"	18.00- 20.00	5.00- 6.00	4.00- 5.00
Plate, 4¼"	9.00- 11.00	4.00- 5.00	3.00- 4.00
Saucer, 3-1/8"	6.00- 7.00	2.50- 3.00	2.00- 3.00
Sugar and Lid, 1-7/8"	28.00- 30.00	13.00- 15.00	13.00- 15.00
Teapot and Lid, 3¾"	35.00- 40.00	14.00- 16.00	13.00- 15.00
Boxed Set, 21 piece	310.00-340.00	125.00-140.00	105.00-125.00

Refer to page 21 for prices of solid opaque colors.

Interior Panel, Large

Shown in the photograph above are the "Interior Panel" sets commonly referred to as the "luster sets". These pieces have a shinier appearance than most other Akro children's dishes. This green should not be confused with the flat darker green shown on the previous page.

Interior Panel, Large	Pink & Green‡‡ Luster		Azure Blue Yellow Opaque	
Cereal, 3-3/8″	10.00-	11.00	14.00-	16.00
Creamer, 1-3/8″	13.00-	14.00	17.00-	22.00†
Cup, 1-3/8″	8.00-	10.00	19.00-	21.00*
Plate, 4¼″	4.50-	5.50	6.50-	7.50
Saucer, 3-1/8″	2.50-	3.50	4.50-	5.50
Sugar and Lid, 1-7/8″	16.00-	19.00	25.00-	30.00†
Teapot and Lid, 3¾″	20.00-	24.00	42.00-	47.00†
Boxed Set, 21 piece	155.00-	175.00	280.00-	300.00

*Pumpkin 50% less; †Cobalt 50% less; ‡‡Flat green 15% less

Miss America (Akro Agate Co.)

The "Miss America" pattern is probably the rarest of all the Akro toy sets. Sets have been found in white opaque, white opaque with decals, orange and white marbleized, and forest green. Unlike other Akro Agate children's pieces, the cup is footed and the open handle is an unusual shape.

Miss America	White*	Orange & White Forest Green
Creamer	25.00- 27.00	32.00- 37.00
Cup	25.00- 27.00	28.00- 30.00
Plate	14.00- 15.00	15.00- 17.00
Saucer	8.00- 10.00	9.00- 12.00
Sugar and Lid	32.00- 37.00	45.00- 47.00
Teapot and Lid	50.00- 55.00	65.00- 70.00
Boxed Set	295.00-325.00	350.00-375.00

*With decal, 50% higher

Octagonal, Large (Akro Agate Co.)

There are two styles of "Octagonal" large sets--open handle and closed handle. The cups, sugar, creamer and teapot come with both open and closed handles. The other pieces in both sets are the same. Open handle "Octagonal" sets are sometimes referred to as "Octagonal-O". "Octagonal" sets come in a wide array of opaque colors. Sets of green and white are among the most easily found of all Akro sets. Therefore the price of these pieces has remained low.

Octagonal, Large	Green/White* Dark Blue	Beige/Pumpkin Light Blue
Cereal, 3-3/8″	3.50- 4.00	-------
‡‡Creamer, closed handle, 1½″	3.00- 3.50	10.00-12.00
‡‡Cup, closed handle, 1½″	1.50- 2.00	8.00-10.00†
Plate, 4¼″	1.50- 2.00	5.00- 7.00
Saucer, 3-3/8″	1.00- 1.25	-------
‡‡Sugar and Lid, closed handle	4.50- 5.00	14.00-15.00
‡‡Teapot and Lid, closed handle, 3-5/8″	7.00- 8.00	14.00-16.00
Boxed Set, 21 piece	44.00-50.00	-------

Octagonal, Large	Lemonade & Oxblood	Pink/Yellow Other Opaques
Cereal, 3-3/8″	20.00- 22.00	5.00- 6.00
Creamer, closed handle, 1½″	20.00- 22.00	4.00- 5.00
Cup, closed handle, 1½″	15.00- 17.00	3.00- 3.50
Plate, 4¼″	8.00- 10.00	2.50- 3.00
Saucer, 3-3/8″	5.00- 6.00	1.50- 2.00
Sugar and Lid, closed handle	25.00- 28.00	6.00- 7.00
Teapot and Lid, closed handle, 3½″	30.00- 35.00	9.00-10.00
Boxed Set, 21 piece	270.00-300.00	70.00-85.00

*Decal, add 50%; †Pumpkin, $20.00; ‡‡Open handle, add 25%.

Octagonal, Small (Akro Agate Co.)

"Octagonal" small sets include a water pitcher and tumblers. The small size open handle cup is found more frequently than the closed handle one. Small-size closed handle teapots, sugars, and creamers have not been found. Since "Octagonal" saucers and small-size "Octagonal" dinner plates are the same size, they are easily confused. However, the saucers have a greater degree of curvature than the dinner plates.

Octagonal, Small	Dark Green Blue/White	Pumpkin/Yellow Lime Green
Creamer, 1¼"	10.00- 12.00★	-------
†Cup, 1¼"	6.00- 8.00	11.00- 13.00
Pitcher	10.00- 12.00★	-------
Plate, 3-3/8"	3.50- 4.00	4.50- 5.50
Saucer, 2¾"	2.00- 3.00	3.00- 5.00
Sugar, 1¼"	10.00- 12.00★	-------
Teapot and Lid, 3-3/8"	12.00- 14.00★	-------
Tumbler, 2"	4.00- 5.00	12.00- 14.00
Boxed Set, 16 Piece	82.00-100.00	-------

★Light and medium blue, 25% less; †Cup, closed handle, add 25%

Raised Daisy (Akro Agate Co.)

"Raised Daisy" sets have been found boxed in 7, 13, and 19 piece sets. Since opaque green cups are found in most boxed sets, blue cups are a welcome addition to any collection. Opaque yellow and beige tumblers are found with embossing. A blue tumbler with no pattern has been found included in a rare nineteen piece boxed set. Three of these sets were found in one old country store.

"Raised Daisy" teapots come in several styles. Of the two lidless styles, only one is embossed. The unembossed style is slightly smaller and thinner; however both have been found boxed as a lemonade pitcher, and a teapot. The third style is shown in the center of the photograph. This teapot has a lid which appears to be a "Stacked Disc" lid. The lid is unique since it will not interchange with either the other styles of "Raised Daisy" teapots or the "Stacked Disc and Panel" teapots.

Raised Daisy	Yellow	Blue	Green	Beige
Creamer, 1-13/16″	25.00-27.00	-------	-------	-------
Cup, 1-13/16″	-------	25.00-27.00	12.00-15.00	-------
Plate, 3″	-------	9.00-11.00	-------	-------
Saucer, 2½″	7.00- 8.00	-------	-------	7.00- 8.00
Sugar, 1-13/16″	25.00-27.00	-------	-------	-------
★Teapot, 2-3/8″	27.00-30.00	20.00-22.00	20.00-22.00	-------
Tumbler, 2″	16.00-18.00	30.00-32.00	-------	16.00-18.00

★Teapot and Lid, blue $45.00-50.00.

Stacked Disc (Akro Agate Co.)

"Stacked Disc" pieces all contain a series of evenly spaced wide horizontal ridges. "Stacked Disc" differs from "Stacked Disc and Interior Panel" since it has a smooth interior surface on the cup, sugar, creamer, teapot, lid, and cereal bowl. The top surface of the saucers and plates is smooth in "Stacked Disc". Small-size pieces are commonly found in green and white opaque. There is also a limited range of other opaque colors. The lack of brilliant color and the inferior quality of the pieces are reasons collectors have shown little interest in this pattern.

Stacked Disc	Opaque Green White	Other Opaque Colors
Creamer, 1¼ "	2.75- 3.00	5.00- 6.00*
Cup, 1¼ "	1.50- 2.00	3.50- 4.00
Pitcher, 2-7/8 "	5.00- 6.00	7.50- 8.50
Plate, 3¼ "	1.50- 1.75	2.50- 3.00
Saucer, 2¾ "	1.50- 1.75	2.50- 3.00
Sugar, 1¼ "	2.75- 3.50	5.00- 6.00*
Teapot and Lid, 3-3/8 "	6.50- 7.50	9.00-10.00*
Tumbler, 2 "	3.00- 4.00	4.00- 5.00*
Boxed Set, 21 Piece	33.00-39.00	58.00-66.00

*Pumpkin 50% higher

Stacked Disc and Interior Panel, Large (Akro Agate Co.)

"Stacked Disc and Interior Panel" pieces have vertical ribs on the interior and concentric horizontal ridges on the exterior. The cereal bowls have the inside panels and a single horizontal rib on the outside.

Akro produced these sets in an exciting array of solid opaque colors, and in the cobalt and green Trans-optic colors. Blue marbleized pieces were also produced, but are almost non-existant. The prices for the opaque colors may seem high, however this set is also difficult to complete.

Large-size sets include a cereal bowl and covered sugar. These teapots and lids, sugars, and creamers will also be found in "Concentric Ring" sets.

Stacked Disc & Interior Panel, Large	Solid Opaque Colors	Blue Marbleized	Transparent Green	Transparent Cobalt
Cereal, 3-3/8"	14.00- 16.00	27.00- 29.00	15.00- 17.00	18.00- 20.00
Creamer, 1-3/8"	10.00- 12.00	25.00- 27.00	14.00- 15.00	22.00- 25.00
Cup, 1-3/8"	13.00- 15.00	24.00- 26.00	13.00- 15.00	16.00- 18.00
Plate, 4¾"	6.00- 7.00	10.00- 12.00	8.00- 10.00	9.00- 10.00
Saucer, 3-1/8"	4.00- 5.00	9.00- 10.00	6.00- 7.00	7.00- 8.00
Sugar and Lid, 1-7/8"	16.00- 18.00	37.00- 40.00	23.00- 25.00	30.00- 32.50
Teapot and Lid, 3¾"	30.00- 35.00	45.00- 50.00	32.00- 35.00	35.00- 40.00
Boxed Set, 21 piece	210.00-240.00	395.00-425.00	242.00-275.00	295.00-325.00

27

Stacked Disc and Interior Panel, Large

Stacked Disc and Interior Panel, Small (Akro Agate Co.)

Small-size sets of "Stacked Disc and Interior Panel" do not have cereal bowls or sugar lids. However, a water pitcher and tumbler is available. Although the water pitcher is easily distinguished from a lidless teapot, collectors often confuse these two pieces. The pattern on the teapot continues to the top edge, while the pitcher has a 7/8″ band at the top which does not contain panels. This band is also lacking five horizontal darts found at the top center of the teapot. Also the sides of the pitcher do not slope inwardly as much as those of the teapot. Also confusing is a similarity between the large-size saucer and the small-size dinner plate. For an explanation of the differences refer to "Octagonal," small.

Tumblers are common in the Trans-optic colors, but appear to be elusive in all the opaque colors.

Stacked Disc and Interior Panel, Small

28

Stacked Disc & Interior Panel, Small	Solid Opaque Colors	Blue Marbleized	Transparent Green	Trans Cobalt
Creamer, 1¼"	5.00- 6.00	25.00- 27.00	13.00- 15.00	18.00- 20.00
Cup, 1¼"	9.00-10.00	24.00- 26.00	9.00- 10.00	14.00- 16.00
Pitcher, 2-7/8"	-------	-------	9.00- 10.00	15.00- 18.00
Plate, 3¼"	3.50- 4.50	10.00- 12.00	6.00- 7.00	8.00- 10.00
Saucer, 2¾"	3.00- 3.50	9.00- 10.00	4.00- 5.00	5.00- 6.00
Sugar, 1¼"	5.00- 6.00	25.00- 27.00	13.00- 15.00	18.00- 20.00
Teapot and Lid, 3-3/8"	13.00-15.00	45.00- 50.00	16.00- 17.00	27.00- 30.00
Tumbler, 2"	18.00-20.00	-------	7.00- 8.00	9.00- 10.00
Boxed Set, 8 Piece	50.00-55.00	135.00-150.00	125.00-140.00	175.00-200.00

Stippled Band, Large (Akro Agate Co.)

Pieces of "Stippled Band" are entirely smooth except for a narrow band of raised dots near the top edge of each piece. "Stippled Band" only comes in transparent amber, green and blue. These are commonly referred to as the "Transoptic" colors.

It might be of interest that while most sugar lids will interchange with small-size teapots, this is not true of the "Stippled Band" lids. Although this is a large-size Akro set, cereal bowls have not surfaced.

Stippled Band, Large	Transparent Amber	Transparent Green	Transparent Azure
Creamer, 1½"	12.00- 14.00	5.00- 6.00	20.00- 22.50
Cup, 1½"	8.00- 10.00	4.00- 5.00	15.00- 18.00
Plate, 4¼"	6.00- 7.00	3.50- 4.50	8.00- 10.00
Saucer, 3¼"	4.00- 5.00	1.50- 2.00	8.00- 10.00
Sugar and Lid, 1-7/8"	16.00- 18.00	8.00-10.00	25.00- 30.00
Teapot and Lid, 3¾"	20.00- 22.00	15.00-16.50	35.00- 40.00
Boxed Set, 17 Piece	125.00-150.00	70.00-83.00	210.00-250.00

Stippled Band, Small (Akro Agate Co.)

The small band of raised dots near the edge on the exterior of each piece provides the name "Stippled Band". These sets are available in the Trans-optic colors. A set in transparent deep red has surfaced. Since very little of this color has been found, and the color varies to a great extent, this is believed to have been an experimental color.

Stippling is occasionally found on "Interior Panel" pieces. However, at this time, there appears to be very little collector interest in this variation of "Interior Panel". Therefore "Stippled Interior Panel" is usually collected and priced as "Interior Panel".

Stippled Band, Small	Transparent Amber	Transparent Green
Creamer, 1¼"	5.00- 6.00	4.50- 5.50
Cup, 1¼"	4.00- 5.00	4.00- 4.50
Pitcher, 2-7/8"	7.50- 8.50	7.50- 8.50
Plate, 3¼"	2.75- 3.25	2.50- 3.00
Saucer, 2¾"	1.75- 2.00	1.50- 2.00
Sugar, 1¼"	5.00- 6.00	4.50- 5.50
Teapot and Lid, 3-3/8"	10.00-12.00	8.00-10.00
Tumbler, 1¾"	5.00- 6.00	4.50- 5.50
Boxed Set, 8 piece	35.00-40.00	30.00-35.00

Houzex (Houze Glass Co.)

Since the shape of the cups and saucers and the sugar and creamer strongly resemble that of the "Miss America" pattern, made by Akro Agate, we have placed this set in this section. We believe this set to have been made by the Houze Glass Company of Point Marion, Pennsylvania. These colored clambroth-type pieces are not easily found. Sets were produced in yellow, blue and green.

Houzex	Opaque Green	Opaque Yellow	Opaque Blue
Creamer, 1¾ "	18.00- 20.00	18.00- 20.00	20.00- 22.00
Cup, 1¼ "	18.00- 20.00	18.00- 20.00	20.00- 22.00
Plate, 4 "	8.00- 10.00	8.00- 10.00	10.00- 12.00
Saucer, 3¼ "	6.00- 8.00	6.00- 8.00	6.00- 8.00
Sugar and Lid, 2-7/8 "	25.00- 27.00	25.00- 27.00	27.00- 30.00
Teapot and Lid, 3-3/8 "	32.00- 35.00	35.00- 37.00	40.00- 45.00
Set, 18 piece	205.00-235.00	205.00-235.00	230.00-265.00

Depression Era Glassware

Several American glass companies made child-size counterparts of their regular size "colored dishes." Although they are classified under the heading "depression glass", these sets were produced largely between 1935 and 1940. During these later years the companies may have been searching for innovative ways to rekindle a waning interest in cheap colored, machine-made glassware. Table sets, pastry sets, and baking sets were among the items produced. Some of these may still be found in their original boxes.

Cherry Blossom (Jeannette Glass Company)

Cherry Blossom was produced in transparent pink and delphite between 1932 and 1938. It was listed in catalogues as "Jeannette's Junior Dinner Set."

The pieces have been heavily reproduced in both original colors, and in cobalt, transparent green, and irridized colors. A butter dish has also been fashioned by using a saucer and a cup. The saucer, with the cup ring removed, is used for the base. The lid is an upside down, handleless cup, with a knob applied. The butter dish was not part of the original set. The quality of the new sets is usually poor, and the color is normally lighter than the original pink or delphite.

*Cherry Blossom	Pink	Delphite
Creamer, 2¾"	25.00- 27.50	22.50- 25.00
Cup, 1½"	20.00- 22.00	20.00- 22.00
Plate, 5-7/8"	7.50- 8.50	5.00- 6.00
Saucer, 4½"	4.00- 5.00	4.00- 5.00
Sugar, 2-5/8"	22.50- 25.00	20.00- 22.50
Boxed Set, 14 piece	178.00-200.00	165.00-185.00

*Entire set reproduced

Cherry Blossom, Delphite

Doric and Pansy (Jeannette Glass Company)

This child's set was produced for a short period of time, between 1937 and 1938, in transparent pink and ultramarine. Jeannette called this set their "Pretty Polly Party Dishes." "Doric and Pansy" is one of the more desirable and more elusive depression glass sets. The ultramarine color tends to vary from teal, to a shade of almost green. Therefore, it is difficult to match pieces if they are bought individually.

Doric and Pansy	Pink	Ultramarine
Creamer, 2¾"	25.00- 28.00	28.00- 30.00
Cup, 1½"	23.00- 25.00	23.00- 25.00
Plate, 5-7/8"	6.00- 7.50	6.00- 7.50
Saucer, 4½"	3.00- 4.00	4.00- 5.00
Sugar, 2½"	20.00- 22.00	22.00- 25.00
Boxed Set, 14 piece	178.00-200.00	185.00-210.00

Homespun (Jeannette Glass Company)

Homespun was made in pink and crystal between 1939 and 1940. The pink teapot is hard to find. The teapot lid is even more elusive. Pink sets are more abundant than crystal, but demand a higher price due to their greater desirability among collectors. This set is unusual since it lacks a sugar and creamer. It is also the only true depression set that contains a teapot.

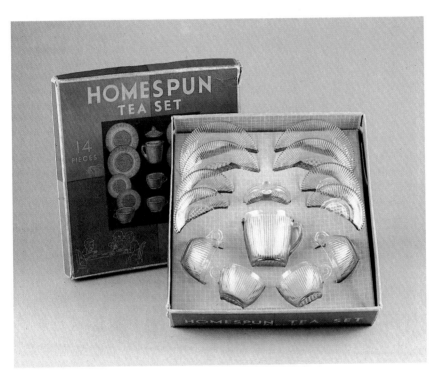

Homespun	Pink	Crystal
Cup, 1-5/8 "	27.00- 29.00	12.00- 14.00
Plate, 4½ "	5.00- 6.00	3.00- 4.00
Saucer, 3¼ "	3.00- 4.00	2.00- 3.00
Teapot and Lid, 3¾ "	47.50- 52.50	-------
Boxed Set, 14 piece	192.50-212.50	-------
Boxed Set, 12 piece	-------	70.00- 85.00

Laurel (McKee Glass Co.)

The Laurel child's tea set was produced in the early 1930's. The boxed sets are marked "Hostess Tea Set--Useful Dishes." McKee made the sets in French ivory and jade green. Some pieces are found with a Scottie dog decal, while others have decorated rims. The plain sets are difficult to complete, and the decorated pieces have become almost impossible to find.

Laurel	French★ Ivory	Jade Green	Scottie Decal
Creamer, 2-5/8 "	20.00- 22.00	22.00- 25.00	32.50- 35.00
Cup, 1½ "	20.00- 22.00	22.00- 25.00	28.00- 30.00
Plate, 5-7/8 "	7.00- 8.00	7.50- 8.50	12.00- 14.00
Saucer, 4-3/8 "	4.00- 5.00	4.50- 5.50	4.50- 5.50
Sugar, 2-3/8 "	18.00- 20.00	20.00- 22.00	32.50- 35.00
Boxed Set, 14 piece	167.00-185.00	185.00-205.00	250.00-275.00

★Decorated trim, add 25%

Laurel

Moderntone (Hazel Atlas Co.)

Hazel Atlas referred to these children's pieces as the "Little Hostess Party Set." The boxes stated, "A Sierra set just like Mothers." The pieces were made of platonite--a type of heat resistant glass. Hazel Atlas made Moderntone during the 1940's and early 1950's. These sets were boxed in a variety of plain and multicolored, fired-on combinations. The dark-color sets include 4 cups, 4 saucers, 4 dinner plates, a sugar, creamer, and a teapot and lid. Pastel sets were sold without a teapot; however a pastel yellow teapot has been found. An unusual platonite set which includes an all white teapot has also been discovered.

Most of the sets contain four colors. There are a few exceptions. Sets in solid white, black and white, and dark pink and black exist. Pastel sets include one of each piece in light green, light yellow, light blue, and light pink. The sugar and creamer are light pink.

Dark-color sets have one of each piece in the following color combinations:
1. Orange, gold, grey, turquoise; orange sugar, creamer; turquoise teapot.
2. Beige, turquoise, lemon yellow, rose; rose sugar, creamer; beige teapot with lemon yellow lid.
3. Dark green, maroon, grey, chartreuse; chartreuse sugar, creamer; maroon teapot.

We have seen the above sets mixed in various other color combinations, but we are unable to confirm them in original boxes.

Moderntone	Pastel Colors	Dark Colors
Creamer, 1¾"	3.00- 3.50	3.25- 3.75
Cup, 1¾"	2.50- 3.00	2.75- 3.25
Plate, 5¼"	2.00- 2.50	2.75- 3.25
Saucer, 3-7/8"	1.00- 1.50	2.25- 2.75
Sugar, 1¾"	3.00- 3.50	3.25- 3.75
Teapot and Lid, 3½"	-------	25.00-30.00
Boxed Set, 14 piece	33.00-40.00	-------
Boxed Set, 16 piece	-------	56.00-60.00
White set, add 20%		

20th Century Set (Hazel Atlas Co.)

As in the Moderntone sets, these sets were also referred to as "Little Hostess Party Sets." They were probably a later issue with a "New Century" look. The sets only came in mixed pastel colors. A gold-decorated cup and saucer is pictured on the right. This was part of a demitasse set.

Creamer	2.50- 3.00
Cup	2.00- 2.50
Plate	1.50- 2.00
Saucer	1.00- 1.25
Sugar	2.50- 3.00
Boxed Set, 4 place	25.00-35.00

Fry Bake Set (Fry Glass Co.)

This set was advertised in a 1922 Good Housekeeping magazine as the "Little Mother's Kidibake Set." It consisted of a miniature casserole and cover, bread baker, pie plate, and two ramekins. The six piece set sold for $2.50. The grill plate pictured is a luncheon size and is ideal for a child to use. This plate has also been found in pink and green.

"Kidibake Set"

Bread Baker, #1928-5	18.00- 20.00	Ramekin, #1923-2½	12.00- 14.00
Casserole, covered,		Set, 6 piece	90.00-105.00
#1938-4½	30.00- 35.00	Plate, grill, 8½"	25.00- 27.50
Pie Plate, #1916-5	18.00- 20.00		

Glasbake "Betty Jane Set" (McKee Glass Co.)

The pieces in this set are similar to those in the Fry set. The measurements are the same for both sets. No red trim, 20% less.

"Betty Jane Set"

Bowl (ramekin), #294	5.50- 6.50	Casserole, covered, #209	22.00-24.00
Bread Baker, rectangular,		Pie Plate, (not shown)	8.00-10.00
#256	12.00-14.00	Set, 6 piece	53.00-60.00

Glasbake "Betty Jane Baking Set" (McKee Glass Co.)

This set consists of nine pieces of heat resisting oven ware. With the exception of the covered casserole, pieces out of the box have little value.

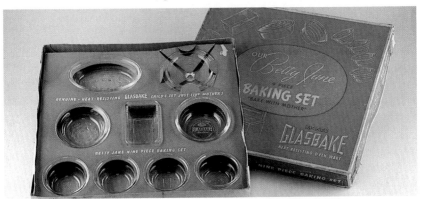

Baker, oval (075),			Casserole, covered	
4¼"x6-3/8"	3.00- 4.00		(064), 3-1/8"	18.00-20.00
Bowl (58), 3-5/8"	1.00- 1.50		Pie Plate (97), 4½"	2.00- 2.50
Bread Baker (025), 3"x4½"	2.50- 3.50		Boxed Set, 9 Piece	35.00-40.00

Fireking "Sunny Suzy Baking Set No. 261" (Anchor Hocking)

This delightful little set was made during the 1940's for Wolverine Supply and Manufacturing Company. The glass pieces were made by Anchor Hocking. Since they used the same pieces from their regular baking line, collectors are only interested in boxed sets. The set is shown in a 1946 Spiegel catalog.

Baker, 2-handle, 10 oz.	3.00- 3.50	Pastry Board	2.50- 3.50
Custard Cup, 5 oz.	1.75- 2.25	Rolling Pin	2.00- 3.00
Dish, deep pie, 5-3/8"	5.00- 5.50	Boxed Set, 8 piece	35.00-40.00

Miscellaneous Depression Items

The above items were made in the 1930's and 1940's. The child's mixer is marked "Delta Detroit." With it are Glasbake mixing bowls.

The beater on the left is Glasbake. The base was also used as an egg cup. The beater on the right is marked "Betty Taplin."

The remainder of the pieces are part of a "Little Deb" series. The ribbed bowl in the foreground is inscribed "Little Deb Toys," and was probably a promotional item. The tumblers, tray, and pitcher are a lemonade set. The glass pieces in this set were made by Hazel Atlas for the Northwestern Products Company. This set was sold as the "Little Deb Lemonade Server Set No. 207." Retail price in a 1946 Spiegel catalog was 89ᶜ.

Beater, left (Glasbake), 6-3/8″	22.00-25.00
Beater, right (Betty Taplin), 6-1/8″	25.00-27.00
Bowl, Glasbake, 3-5/8″	1.00- 1.50
Bowl, ribbed (Little Deb), 3-1/8″	10.00-12.00
Mixer (Delta Detroit), 5″	18.00-20.00
Pitcher, 3-7/8″	3.50- 4.00
Tumbler, 2-1/8″	2.00- 2.50
Boxed Lemonade Set	20.00-25.00

Pattern Glass

Pressed glass toy dishes were prolifically produced by many glass companies during the last half of the 19th century and in the early years of the 20th century. Many of these companies were located in the western Pennsylvania, eastern Ohio, and West Virginia areas, because of the abundant supply of cheap natural gas.

Several types of sets were produced, but not all pieces were available in every pattern. Included were table sets, water sets, punch sets, berry sets, vegetable sets and stein sets. A table set consists of a covered butter, a covered sugar, a creamer, and a spooner. The punch set includes a punch bowl and six punch cups. The water set has a pitcher and six tumblers. The berry set consists of a large berry and six small berries. The vegetable set is shown in a Federal Glass Company catalog. It is only known in the "Tulip and Honeycomb" pattern and is composed of four pieces. These include a round covered dish, an oval covered dish, a round open dish, and an oval open dish. Stein sets consist of a large stein and six small steins. Other special pieces such as candlesticks, mugs, or cups and saucers were made in a few patterns.

The Sandwich glass shown on page 91 was made by the Sandwich Glass Company of Sandwich, Massachusetts. The "lacy" miniatures were produced between 1825 and 1840. When demand dropped for this type of glass, the company started producing "panelled" pieces. These were made until 1888, when the company closed. Several attempts were made to reopen the factory between 1888 and 1900, but none were successful.

Acorn

	Crystal
Butter, 4″	145.00-155.00
Creamer, 3-3/8″	72.00- 77.00
Spooner, 3-1/8″	72.00- 77.00
Sugar and Lid, 4¾″	120.00-130.00
Table Set	410.00-440.00

Arched Panel (Westmoreland Glass Co.)

	Crystal	Amber	Cobalt
Pitcher	18.00-20.00	74.00- 76.00	74.00- 76.00
Tumbler	6.00- 8.00	18.00- 20.00	21.00- 23.00
★Water Set, 7 piece	54.00-68.00	182.00-196.00	200.00-214.00

★Reproduced in crystal and colors

Austrian No. 200 (Greentown)

	Crystal	Canary	Chocolate
Butter, 2¼"	170.00-180.00	290.00-310.00	640.00- 660.00
Creamer, 3¼"	70.00- 80.00	145.00-155.00	235.00- 255.00
Spooner, 3"	70.00- 80.00	145.00-155.00	245.00- 260.00
Sugar and Lid, 3¾"	120.00-130.00	240.00-260.00	440.00- 470.00
Table Set	430.00-470.00	820.00-880.00	1,560.00-1,645.00

Baby Thumbprint (United States Glass Co.)

A butter dish has been authenticated in a United States Glass Company catalogue, dated 1915.

	Crystal
Cakestand, tall, 3"	67.00- 70.00
Cakestand, short, 2"	75.00- 80.00
Compote, covered	110.00-120.00
Compote, flared rim (no cover)	140.00-150.00

Bead and Scroll

Dark green and dark blue pieces have been reported.

	Crystal
Butter, 4"	145.00-150.00
Creamer, 3"	50.00- 65.00
Spooner, 2¾"	50.00- 65.00
Sugar and Lid, 4"	70.00- 95.00
Table Set	325.00-375.00

Beaded Swirl (Westmoreland Glass Co.)

	Crystal*		Crystal*
Butter, 2-3/8"	47.00- 52.00	Sugar and Lid, 3¾"	39.00- 42.00
Creamer, 2¾"	27.00- 30.00	Table Set	140.00-154.00
Spooner, 2¼"	27.00- 30.00		

*Cobalt, amber, double price

"Block"
A creamer has been found in blue milk glass. Hopefully other pieces will surface.

	Crystal	Amber	Blue	Blue Milk glass
Butter, 3"	122.00-127.00	130.00-140.00	135.00-140.00	
Creamer, 3"	47.00- 50.00	50.00- 55.00	50.00- 55.00	85.00- 90.00
Spooner, 3"	50.00- 55.00	55.00- 60.00	55.00- 60.00	
Sugar and Lid, 4½"	85.00- 95.00	95.00-100.00	95.00-100.00	
Table Set	305.00-325.00	330.00-355.00	335.00-355.00	

Braided Belt

	Crystal	White/ Decorated
Butter, 2¼"	95.00-110.00	240.00-260.00
Creamer, 2-5/8"	45.00- 50.00	95.00-100.00
Spooner, 2-5/8"	50.00- 55.00	95.00-105.00
Sugar, 2-5/8"	75.00- 86.00	140.00-160.00
Table Set	265.00-290.00	570.00-625.00

Bucket "Wooden Pail" (Bryce Brothers)

	Crystal
Butter, 2¼"	200.00-210.00
Creamer, 2½"	50.00- 60.00
Spooner, 2½"	100.00-110.00
Sugar and Lid, 3¾"	160.00-170.00
Table Set	510.00-550.00

Button Panel No. 44 (George Duncan's Sons and Co.)

	Crystal	Crystal/ Gold
Butter, 4"	75.00- 77.00	80.00- 85.00
Creamer, 2½"	40.00- 45.00	45.00- 50.00
Spooner, 2-9/16"	40.00- 45.00	50.00- 55.00
Sugar and Lid, 4-5/8"	70.00- 75.00	70.00- 80.00
Table Set	230.00-240.00	245.00-270.00

Buzz Saw (Cambridge Glass Co.)

	Crystal
Butter, 2-3/8"	27.00- 30.00
Creamer, 2-3/8"	19.00- 21.00
Spooner, 2-1/8"	20.00- 22.00
Sugar and Lid, 2-7/8"	27.00- 30.00
Table Set	93.00-112.00

Chimo

	Crystal
Butter, 2-3/8"	65.00- 70.00
*Creamer, 2"	35.00- 40.00
*Spooner, 2-1/8"	45.00- 50.00
Sugar and Lid, 3"	55.00- 60.00
Table Set	200.00-220.00
Punch Cup, 1-7/16"	14.00- 16.00

*Reproduced in crystal and colors

Clear and Diamond Panels

	Crystal	**Green**	**Blue**
Butter, 2-7/8"	45.00- 50.00	55.00- 60.00	60.00- 65.00
Creamer, 2¾"	20.00- 22.00	30.00- 35.00	32.00- 37.00
Spooner, 2¼"	22.00- 25.00	30.00- 35.00	32.00- 37.00
Sugar and Lid, 3½"	35.00- 40.00	40.00- 45.00	45.00- 50.00
Table Set	122.00-137.00	155.00-175.00	170.00-190.00

Cloud Band (Gillinder and Sons, Inc.)

	Crystal	White Milk glass
Butter, 3¾"	100.00-110.00	145.00-155.00
Creamer, 2½"	30.00- 35.00	40.00- 45.00
Spooner, 2-3/8"	30.00- 35.00	40.00- 45.00
Sugar and Lid, 4"	60.00- 70.00	90.00- 95.00
Table Set	220.00-250.00	315.00-340.00

Colonial

	Crystal
Pitcher, 3¼"	15.00- 17.00
Tumbler, 2"	4.00- 5.00
Water Set	40.00- 47.00
Punch Bowl, 3-3/16"	35.00- 40.00
Punch Cup, 1-7/8"	13.00- 14.00
Punch Set	110.00-125.00

Colonial No. 2630 (Cambridge Glass Co.)

	Crystal	Olive and Emerald Green	Cobalt
Butter, 2½"	20.00- 22.00	47.00- 52.00	50.00- 55.00
Creamer, 2-3/8"	15.00- 17.00	30.00- 35.00	35.00- 40.00
Spooner, 2-1/8"	17.00- 19.00	35.00- 40.00	40.00- 45.00
Sugar and Lid, 3"	18.00- 20.00	40.00- 45.00	45.00- 50.00
Table Set	70.00- 78.00	150.00-170.00	170.00-190.00

Dewdrop "Hobnail with Hobnail Base" (Columbia Glass Co.)

	Crystal*
Butter, 2-5/8"	95.00-105.00
Creamer, 2¾"	50.00- 60.00
Spooner, 2¾"	60.00- 70.00
Sugar and Lid, 4-1/8"	80.00- 90.00
Table Set	285.00-325.00

*Blue, amber, add 50%

51

Diamond Ridge "D&M #48"

	Crystal
Butter	150.00-160.00
Creamer, 2½"	70.00- 75.00
Spooner, 2¾"	55.00- 60.00
Sugar and Lid, 4-5/8"	120.00-130.00
Table Set	400.00-425.00

Doyle No. 500 (Doyle and Co.)

	Crystal	Amber*	Blue
Butter, 2¼"	45.00- 55.00	80.00- 85.00	85.00- 90.00
Creamer, 2½"	30.00- 32.00	55.00- 60.00	55.00- 60.00
Spooner, 2¼"	30.00- 32.00	55.00- 60.00	55.00- 60.00
Sugar and Lid, 3-5/8"	40.00- 45.00	70.00- 75.00	75.00- 80.00
Tray, 6-5/8"	22.00- 25.00	40.00- 45.00	40.00- 45.00
Table Set	167.00-180.00	300.00-325.00	310.00-335.00
Mug, 2"	20.00- 22.00	35.00- 37.00	37.00- 40.00

*Canary, add 20%

Drum

	Crystal		Crystal
Butter, 2¼"	94.00- 98.00	Table Set	315.00-330.00
Creamer, 2¾"	62.00- 67.00	*Mug, 2-3/16"	18.00- 20.00
Spooner, 2-5/8"	67.00- 70.00	Mug, 2½"	29.00- 32.00
Sugar and Lid,		Mug, 2"	33.00- 35.00
3½"	92.00- 97.00		

*Reproduced

D&M No. 42 (Duncan and Miller Co.)

	Crystal*		Crystal*
Butter, 4"	90.00-100.00	Honey Jug, 2-3/8"	60.00- 65.00
Creamer, 2-5/8"	33.00- 37.00	Table Set	290.00-325.00
Spooner, 2-9/16"	35.00- 40.00	Rose Bowl, 2-1/8"	62.00- 67.00
Sugar and Lid, 4½"	70.00- 80.00		

*Gold decorated, add 10%

"Dutch Kinder"

	White Milk glass	Blue Milk glass	Apple Green	Crystal
Bowl, 1-3/16"	75.00- 77.00	85.00- 90.00	-------	-------
Candlestick, 3"	75.00- 80.00	110.00-125.00	75.00-85.00	-------
Chamber Pot, 2-1/8"	65.00- 70.00	75.00- 85.00	-------	-------
Pitcher, 2¼"	75.00- 80.00	85.00- 90.00	-------	-------
Pomade, 1½"	85.00- 90.00	85.00- 90.00	-------	90.00-95.00
Slop Jar, 2-1/8"	75.00- 77.00	75.00- 77.00	-------	-------
Tray, 3¾"x6"	105.00-110.00	125.00-130.00	-------	-------

Fancy Cut (Rex) (Co-Operative Flint Glass Co.)

	Crystal		Crystal
*Butter, 2-3/8"	32.00- 36.00	Tumbler, 1-5/8"	17.00- 18.00
Creamer, 2¼"	21.00- 23.00	Water Set	137.00-145.00
Spooner, 2¼"	21.00- 23.00	Punch Bowl,	
Sugar and Lid, 3-1/8"	34.00- 37.00	4-3/8"	70.00- 75.00
Table Set	108.00-120.00	Punch Cup, 1¼"	21.00- 23.00
Pitcher, 3½"	35.00- 37.00	Punch Set	215.00-230.00

*Teal butter, $150.00-175.00

54

Fernland No. 2635 (Cambridge Glass Co.)

	Crystal	Olive and Emerald Green	Cobalt
Butter, 2-5/8"	20.00- 22.00	50.00- 54.00	55.00- 60.00
Creamer, 2-3/8"	15.00- 18.00	35.00- 40.00	37.00- 40.00
Spooner, 2-3/8"	17.00- 19.00	35.00- 40.00	37.00- 40.00
Sugar and Lid, 3"	18.00- 20.00	40.00- 45.00	48.00- 52.00
Table Set	70.00- 80.00	155.00-175.00	165.00-190.00

Fine Cut

	Crystal
Master Berry, 1¾"	60.00- 65.00
Small Berry, 7/8"	8.00- 9.00
Berry Set	110.00-120.00

Flute

	Crystal	Crystal with Gold
Master Berry	20.00-22.00	47.00- 52.00
Small Berry	5.50- 6.50	20.00- 25.00
Berry Set	53.00-58.00	167.00-200.00

Frances Ware (Hobbs, Brockunier and Co.)

	Crystal with Amber Blue or Vaseline	Frosted with Amber Frosted with Red
Pitcher, 4¾"	90.00- 95.00	95.00-100.00
Tumbler, 2¼"	45.00- 50.00	47.00- 50.00
Water Set	360.00-395.00	375.00-400.00

Galloway

	Crystal	Crystal with Gold	Blush
Pitcher, 3-7/8"	19.00- 21.00	22.00- 24.00	65.00- 70.00
Tumbler, 2"	5.50- 6.50	9.00- 11.00	15.00- 17.00
Water Set	52.00- 57.00	75.00- 90.00	155.00-170.00

Grapevine with Ovals (McKee)

	Crystal
Butter, 1½"	72.00- 77.00
*Creamer, 2"	62.00- 67.00
Spooner, 1-7/8"	35.00- 40.00
Sugar and Lid, 2-7/8"	38.00- 42.00
Table Set	205.00-225.00

*Amber, blue, yellow $50.00

Hawaiian Lei

	Crystal
*Butter, 2¼"	35.00- 37.00
*Creamer, 2"	15.00- 17.00
Spooner, 2¼"	24.00- 27.00
*Sugar and Lid, 3"	19.00- 22.00
Table Set	93.00-103.00
Cake Plate	35.00- 45.00

*Reproduced in clear, light blue, pink, cobalt

Hobnail With Thumbprint Base No. 150 (Doyle and Co.)

	Crystal	Blue Amber
Butter, 2"	67.00- 72.00	82.00- 87.00
Creamer, 3-3/8"	30.00- 34.00	35.00- 37.00
Spooner, 2-7/8"	38.00- 42.00	54.00- 56.00
Sugar and Lid, 4"	58.00- 62.00	78.00- 83.00
Tray, 7-3/8"	25.00- 30.00	38.00- 42.00
Table Set	220.00-240.00	285.00-305.00

Horizontal Threads

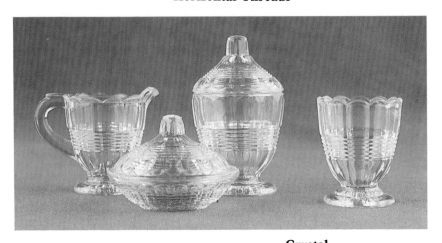

	Crystal
Butter, 1-7/8″	47.00- 52.00
Creamer, 2¼″	24.00- 26.00
Spooner, 2-1/8″	24.00- 26.00
Sugar and Lid, 3-3/8″	38.00- 42.00
Table Set	133.00-145.00

Red flashed, add 20%

Inverted Strawberry (Cambridge Glass Co.)

	Crystal
Master Berry, 1-5/8″	60.00- 65.00
Small Berry, ½″	19.00- 22.00
Berry Set	174.00-197.00
*Punch Bowl, 3-3/8″	47.00- 52.00
*Punch Cup, 1-1/8″	18.00- 20.00
Punch Set	155.00-172.00

*Reproduced in crystal and colors by Mosser Glass Co.; Marked "M"

59

"Kittens" (Fenton)

Some variations of these pieces are currently being made by Fenton in aqua, opalescent, and red.

	Marigold	**Blue**
Banana Dish	105.00-115.00	
Bowl, cereal, 3½"	90.00- 95.00	
Bowl, ruffled, 4 point, 4½"	110.00-115.00	
Bowl, ruffled, 6 point, 4¼"	130.00-145.00	
Vase, ruffled, 2-3/8"	105.00-115.00	
Cup, 2-1/8"	85.00- 90.00	110.00-120.00
Saucer, 4½"	45.00- 50.00	60.00- 65.00

Lamb

	Crystal*
†Butter, 3-1/8"	105.00-110.00
†Creamer, 2-7/8"	57.00- 62.00
Spooner, 2-1/8"	83.00- 87.00
†Sugar and Lid, 4-1/8"	95.00-105.00
Table Set	340.00-365.00

*White milkglass, add 50%
†Reproduced in carnival colors and white milkglass

Liberty Bell (Gillinder and Sons)

	Crystal*		Crystal*
Butter, 2¼"	170.00-180.00	Sugar and Lid, 3-5/8"	125.00-135.00
Creamer, 2½"	70.00- 75.00	Table Set	455.00-490.00
Spooner, 2-3/8"	90.00-100.00	Mug, 2"	100.00-125.00

*White milkglass, double price

Lion (Gillinder and Sons)

	Crystal	Frosted	Crystal with Frosted Head
Butter, 4¼"	90.00-100.00	135.00-140.00	150.00-160.00
Creamer, 3-1/8"	62.00- 68.00	75.00- 80.00	80.00- 85.00
Spooner, 3"	82.00- 87.00	90.00- 95.00	100.00-110.00
Sugar and Lid, 4¼"	90.00- 95.00	110.00-115.00	120.00-125.00
Table Set	325.00-350.00	410.00-425.00	450.00-480.00
Cup, 1-11/16"	35.00- 40.00		
Saucer, 3¼"	15.00- 20.00		

Long Diamond No. 15006 (U.S. Glass Co.)

	Crystal
Butter, 2"	120.00-130.00
Creamer, 2-7/8"	42.00- 47.00
Spooner, 2½"	60.00- 65.00
Sugar and Lid, 3-7/8"	90.00-100.00
Table Set	310.00-340.00

Menagerie (Bryce, Higbee Co.)

	Crystal	Amber	Blue
Butter, 2-3/8"	520.00-530.00	810.00- 850.00	725.00- 750.00
Creamer, 3¾"	75.00- 85.00	120.00- 130.00	110.00- 120.00
Spooner, 2-5/8"	75.00- 85.00	120.00- 130.00	110.00- 120.00
*Sugar and Lid, 4¼"	240.00-260.00	350.00- 375.00	325.00- 350.00
Table Set	910.00-960.00	1,400.00-1,485.00	1,270.00-1,340.00

*Sugar lid does not have a slot

Michigan (U.S. Glass Co.)

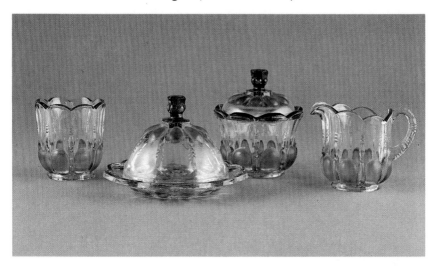

	Crystal	Crystal with Gold	Crystal Flashed Red & Green
Butter, 3½"	90.00- 95.00	115.00-120.00	140.00-150.00
Creamer, 2-7/8"	37.00- 42.00	50.00- 55.00	65.00- 70.00
Spooner, 3"	37.00- 42.00	50.00- 55.00	65.00- 70.00
Sugar and Lid, 4¼"	64.00- 68.00	80.00- 86.00	105.00-115.00
Table Set	230.00-250.00	295.00-315.00	375.00-400.00

Nearcut Water Set (Cambridge Glass Co.)

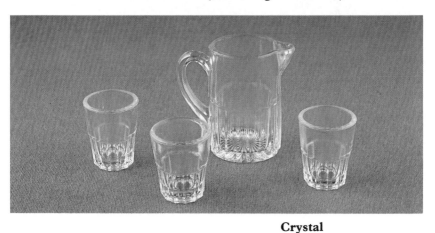

	Crystal
Pitcher, 3-1/8"	28.00-30.00
Tumbler, 2"	5.50- 6.50
Water Set	60.00-70.00

Nursery Rhyme (U.S. Glass Co.)

	Crystal		**Crystal**
Butter, 2-3/8″	65.00- 70.00	Small Berry,	
Creamer, 2½″	37.00- 42.00	1¼″x2½″	18.00- 20.00
Spooner, 2½″	37.00- 42.00	Berry Set, 7 Piece	160.00-180.00
Sugar and Lid,		Pitcher, 4¼″	70.00- 75.00
3-7/8″	65.00- 70.00	Tumbler, 2″	18.00- 20.00
Table Set	200.00-225.00	Water Set, 7 Piece	180.00-195.00
Master Berry,			
1¼″x4¼″	50.00- 60.00		

Nursery Rhyme (U.S. Glass Co.)

	Crystal	**White Milk glass**	**Blue Milk glass**	**Cobalt**
Punch Bowl, 3¼″	80.00- 90.00	120.00-130.00	240.00-260.00	400.00-425.00
Punch Cup, 1-3/8″	20.00- 22.00	23.00- 25.00	40.00- 45.00	70.00- 75.00
Punch Set, 7 Piece	200.00-220.00	260.00-280.00	480.00-530.00	820.00-875.00

Oval Star No. 300 (Indiana Glass Co.)

	Crystal*		Crystal*
Butter, 3½"	18.00- 19.00	Pitcher, 4"	42.00- 45.00
Creamer, 2½"	12.00- 13.00	Tumbler, 2¼"	8.00- 9.00
Spooner, 2½"	12.00- 13.00	Tray, 7¼"	70.00- 75.00
Sugar and Lid, 4-3/8"	14.00- 15.00	Water Set, 8 Piece	160.00-175.00
Table Set	56.00- 60.00	Master Berry, 2"	28.00- 30.00
Punch Bowl	52.00- 55.00	Small Berry, 1"	8.00- 9.00
Punch Cup	7.50- 8.50	Berry Set, 7 Piece	75.00- 85.00
Punch Set, 7 Piece	97.00-105.00	*Crystal with gold, add 25%	

Pattee Cross (U.S. Glass Co.)

	Crystal*		Crystal*
Master Berry, 1¾"	35.00- 40.00	Punch Cup, 1-1/8"	20.00- 22.00
Small Berry, 1"	10.00- 12.00	Punch Set, 7 piece	195.00-210.00
Berry Set, 7 piece	95.00-110.00	Pitcher, 4½"	40.00- 45.00
Punch Bowl	75.00- 80.00	Tumbler, 1¾"	12.00- 14.00
*Crystal with gold, add 25%		Water Set, 7 piece	110.00-130.00

Peacock Feather (U.S. Glass Co.)

	Crystal
Cakestand, 3"	75.00-85.00
Creamer, 2"	45.00-50.00

Pennsylvania (U.S. Glass Co.)

	Crystal*	**Green**
Butter, 3½"	75.00- 85.00	140.00-150.00
Creamer, 2½"	37.00- 40.00	70.00- 75.00
Spooner, 2½"	37.00- 40.00	70.00- 75.00
Sugar and Lid, 4"	60.00- 65.00	115.00-120.00
Table Set	210.00-225.00	395.00-420.00

*With gold, add 25%

Pert

	Crystal
Butter, 2¾ "	120.00-125.00
Creamer, 3¼ "	80.00- 85.00
Spooner, 3 "	120.00-125.00
Sugar and Lid, 5-1/8 "	135.00-140.00
Table Set	455.00-475.00

Plain Pattern No. 13 (King Glass Co.)

	Crystal*	White Milk glass	Cobalt
Butter, 1-7/8 "	67.00- 70.00	105.00-110.00	140.00-150.00
Creamer, 2¼ "	38.00- 40.00	65.00- 68.00	85.00- 90.00
Spooner, 2-3/16 "	42.00- 45.00	70.00- 73.00	90.00- 95.00
Sugar and Lid, 3¼ "	55.00- 57.00	80.00- 85.00	110.00-120.00
Table Set	200.00-210.00	320.00-335.00	425.00-455.00

*Crystal with frosted panels, add 50%

"Rooster" No. 140 (King Glass Co.)

	Crystal
Butter, 2¾"	120.00-130.00
Creamer, 3¼"	80.00- 85.00
Nappy	100.00-110.00
Spooner, 3"	120.00-130.00
Sugar and Lid, 5"	130.00-140.00
Table Set	450.00-485.00

Sandwich Ivy

	Crystal	**Amethyst**
Creamer, 2-3/8"	70.00-80.00	90.00-100.00
Sugar, 3¼"	70.00-80.00	90.00-100.00

Sawtooth

	Crystal
Butter, 3"	47.50- 50.00
Creamer, 3½"	30.00- 32.00
Spooner, 3¼"	32.00- 35.00
Sugar and Lid, 4-7/8"	37.00- 40.00
Table Set	145.00-157.00

Sawtooth Band No. 1225 (A.H. Heisey and Co.)

	Crystal	**Red Flashed**
Butter, 3-7/8"	145.00-155.00	210.00-220.00
Creamer, 2½"	45.00- 55.00	65.00- 70.00
Spooner, 2¼"	45.00- 50.00	65.00- 70.00
Sugar and Lid, 4-1/8"	95.00-105.00	140.00-150.00
Table Set	330.00-365.00	480.00-510.00

Sawtooth "Variation"

	Crystal		Crystal
Butter, 4″	57.00- 60.00	Sugar and Lid, 5″	42.00- 47.00
Creamer, 3¾″	28.00- 30.00	Table Set	160.00-170.00
Spooner, 3″	32.00- 35.00		

Standing Lamb

	Crystal	Frosted
Butter	250.00- 275.00	275.00- 300.00
Creamer, 3¼″	190.00- 210.00	275.00- 300.00
Spooner	250.00- 275.00	285.00- 300.00
Sugar and Lid, 5-1/8″	250.00- 275.00	285.00- 300.00
Table Set	940.00-1,035.00	1,070.00-1,200.00

Stippled Raindrop and Dewdrop

	Crystal	Amber Cobalt
Butter, 1¾"	70.00- 75.00	125.00-130.00
Creamer, 2¼"	52.00- 55.00	92.00- 97.00
Spooner, 2-1/8"	55.00- 57.00	97.00-102.00
Sugar and Lid, 3"	60.00- 65.00	105.00-110.00
Table Set	235.00-250.00	420.00-440.00

Stippled Diamond

	Crystal	Blue Amber
Butter, 2¼"	70.00- 75.00	105.00-110.00
Creamer, 2¼"	57.00- 60.00	85.00- 90.00
Spooner, 2-1/8"	57.00- 60.00	85.00- 90.00
Sugar and Lid, 3-1/8"	70.00- 75.00	105.00-110.00
Table Set	225.00-270.00	380.00-400.00

"Stippled Vines and Beads"

	Crystal	Teal Amber	Saphire Blue
Butter, 2-3/8"	70.00- 75.00	100.00-110.00	110.00-115.00
Creamer, 2-3/8"	55.00- 60.00	85.00- 90.00	90.00- 95.00
Spooner, 2-1/8"	57.00- 60.00	85.00- 90.00	90.00- 95.00
Sugar and Lid, 3-1/8"	70.00- 75.00	100.00-110.00	110.00-115.00
Table Set	250.00-270.00	370.00-400.00	400.00-420.00

Sultan (McKee Glass Co.)

Sultan comes with both a plain and a stippled background. The stippled type is not easily found.

	Crystal*	Green/Green Frosted	Chocolate
Butter, 3¾"	100.00-105.00	125.00-130.00	500.00- 525.00
Creamer, 2½"	55.00- 60.00	70.00- 75.00	250.00- 260.00
Spooner, 2½"	65.00- 70.00	75.00- 80.00	250.00- 260.00
Sugar and Lid, 4½"	95.00-100.00	120.00-125.00	300.00- 320.00
Table Set	315.00-335.00	390.00-410.00	1,300.00-1,365.00

*Crystal frosted, add 10%

Tappan (McKee Glass Co.)

The pieces which have been reproduced are collectible today. They are valued slightly higher than their crystal counterparts.

	Crystal	Colors
*Butter, 3"	27.00-29.00	30.00-35.00
*Creamer, 2-7/8"	14.00-15.00	20.00-22.00
Spooner, 2-5/8"	14.00-15.00	-------
*Sugar and Lid, 4"	17.00-19.00	25.00-27.00
Table Set	72.00-78.00	75.00-84.00

*Reproduced in white milk glass, amethyst, teal, green, red, and amber by Kemple in the late 1950's to mid 1960's.

Tulip and Honeycomb (Federal Glass Co.)

	Crystal		Crystal
Butter, 3-5/8"	35.00- 40.00	Bowl, oval, open, 1¾"	50.00- 55.00
Creamer, 2-5/8"	15.00- 20.00	Bowl, round, open, 1¾"	50.00- 55.00
Spooner, 2½"	15.00- 20.00	Dish, low, covered, 2-3/8"	40.00- 45.00
Sugar and Lid, 3¾"	25.00- 30.00	Casserole, oval, covered,	
Table Set	90.00-100.00	3¼"	70.00- 75.00
Punch Bowl, 4¼"	25.00- 30.00	Casserole, round, covered,	
*Punch Cup, 1¼"	7.00- 9.00	3¼"	70.00- 75.00
Punch Set, 7 piece	67.00- 84.00	Vegetable Set	280.00-305.00
*Also comes in aqua			

"Twin Snowshoes" Sunbeam No. 15139 (U.S. Glass Co.)

	Crystal		Crystal
Butter, 2"	85.00- 90.00	Sugar and Lid, 3-1/8"	55.00- 65.00
Creamer, 2-7/8"	35.00- 40.00	Table Set	215.00-245.00
Spooner, 2-1/8"	40.00- 45.00		

Twist No. 137 (Albany Glass Co.)
The butter lid and sugar lid will interchange.

	Crystal	Frosted	Blue Opalescent	White/ Vaseline Opalescent
Butter, 3-5/8"	25.00-27.00	55.00- 60.00	140.00-145.00	135.00-145.00
Creamer, 2½"	14.00-15.00	50.00- 55.00	85.00- 90.00	80.00- 85.00
Spooner, 2-3/8"	14.00-15.00	40.00- 50.00	85.00- 90.00	80.00- 85.00
Sugar and Lid, 3-7/8"	15.00-17.00	55.00- 60.00	95.00-105.00	90.00-100.00
Table Set	68.00-74.00	200.00-225.00	405.00-430.00	385.00-415.00

Two Band

	Crystal
Butter, 2″	55.00- 60.00
Creamer, 2¾″	25.00- 30.00
Spooner, 2-7/8″	30.00- 35.00
Sugar and Lid, 3¾″	45.00- 50.00
Table Set	155.00-180.00

Wee Branches

	Crystal	
Butter, 1-5/8″	75.00- 85.00	
Creamer, 2-3/16″	35.00- 40.00	
Spooner, 2½″	40.00- 45.00	
Sugar and Lid, 2-7/8″	55.00- 65.00	
Table Set	205.00-235.00	

	Crystal	**Blue**
Cup, 1-5/8″	35.00-40.00	
Saucer, 3″	12.00-15.00	
Mug, 2″	30.00-35.00	40.00-45.00
Plate, 3″	45.00-50.00	

Wheat Sheaf No. 500 (Cambridge Glass Co.)

	Crystal
Master Berry, 2¼"	32.00- 35.00
Small Berry, 1"	7.50- 8.50
Berry Set, 7 piece	77.00- 86.00
Wine Jug, 4-1/8"	50.00- 55.00
Tumbler, 1¾"	18.00- 22.00
Wine Set, 7 piece	160.00-185.00

	Crystal	White Milkglass
Punch Bowl, 3½"	26.00-28.00	
Punch Cup, 1¼"	7.50- 8.50	18.00-20.00
Punch Set, 7 piece	70.00-80.00	

Whirligig No. 15101 (U.S. Glass Co.)

	Crystal		Crystal
Butter, 2½"	19.00-21.00	Table Set	64.00-73.00
Creamer, 2¼"	12.00-15.00	Punch Bowl, 4¾"	25.00-27.00
Spooner, 2¼"	15.00-17.00	*Punch Cup, 1-3/16"	6.00- 7.00
Sugar and Lid, 3¼"	18.00-20.00	Punch Set, 7 piece	61.00-69.00

*Reproduced

Wild Rose (Greentown)

	White Milk glass*	Blue Milk glass
Butter, 3½"	65.00- 75.00	
Creamer, 1¾"	55.00- 60.00	
Spooner, 1¾"	55.00- 60.00	
Sugar, no lid, 1¾"	55.00- 60.00	
Table Set	230.00-255.00	

	White Milk glass	Blue Milk glass
Punch Bowl, 4-1/8"	75.00- 85.00	100.00-110.00
Punch Cup, 1-3/16"	18.00- 20.00	24.00- 26.00
Punch Set	185.00-205.00	240.00-265.00

*Red, blue, gold trim, add 25%

Wild Rose

	Crystal		Crystal
Punch Bowl, 4-1/8"	95.00-100.00	Punch Set	225.00-250.00
Punch Cup, 1-3/16"	22.00- 25.00	Candlestick	75.00- 80.00

Ice Cream Set
Fish Set (Federal Glass Co.)

Although the maker of the "Ice Cream Set" is still unknown, the similar "Fish Set" has been identified as a Federal Glass Company product. A plate from the "Fish Set" is pictured in the foreground.

	Ice Cream Set	Fish Set
Plate, 2¾"	35.00- 40.00	70.00- 80.00
Platter, 4½"x5¾"	125.00-135.00	200.00-225.00
Set, 7 piece	335.00-375.00	620.00-700.00

"Monk" Toy Stein Set

Some sets in white milk glass are flashed with various colors, or trimmed with gold. Pieces came with or without rings at the top, but crystal sets have only been found with rings. These sets were advertised in a 1910 Butler Brothers' catalogue as a "Toy Stein Set."

	Crystal/White Milk glass		Crystal/White Milk glass
Stein, 2"	25.00- 27.00	Set, 5 Piece	170.00-195.00
Tankard, 4"	70.00- 80.00		

Cups and Saucers

Top Row: 1. Cat and Dog, Amber $75.00-85.00; Crystal $50.00-55.00; Blue $75.00-85.00.
Bottom Row: 1. Lion $60.00-65.00. 2. Opal Lace $40.00-45.00.

Mugs

Top Row: 1. "Banded Block," amber $28.00-30.00; 2. Stippled Forget-Me-Not, crystal $45.00-50.00; 3. "Beaded Arrow," crystal $24.00-27.00; 4. "Cat-at-Play," amber $45.00-50.00.
Center Row: 1. Wee Branches, blue $35.00-40.00; 2. Drum, 2", crystal $33.00-35.00; 3. Sawtooth, amber $28.00-30.00; 4. Sawtooth, blue $28.00-30.00; 5. Grapevine with Ovals, crystal $25.00-28.00.
Bottom Row: 1. "Short Panel," blue $18.00-20.00; 2. "Bead and Shield," blue milk glass $30.00-35.00; 3. "Bead and Dart," blue $15.00-18.00.

Mugs

Top Row: 1. Fighting Cats, crystal $38.00-40.00; 2. "Pups and Chicks," amber $50.00-55.00; 3. "Pups and Chicks," vaseline $55.00-60.00; 4. Cupid and Venus, crystal $52.00-57.00; 5. Hook, crystal $20.00-22.00.

Center Row: 1. Lighthouse, crystal $32.00-35.00; 2. Thousand Eye, vaseline $55.00-60.00; 3. Thousand Eye, amber $47.00-50.00; 4. Doyle No. 500, crystal $30.00-35.00; 5. Doyle No. 500, blue $35.00-40.00.

Bottom Row: 1. Begging Dog, crystal $50.00-55.00; 2. Panelled, blue $35.00-40.00; 3. Liberty Bell, crystal $100.00-105.00.

Mugs

Top Row: 1. Drum, 2½", crystal $29.00-32.00; 2. "School Children," crystal $47.00-50.00; 3. Drum 2-3/16", crystal $18.00-20.00; 4. Ribbed Forget-Me-Not, crystal $18.00-20.00.

Center Row: 1. "School Children," blue $70.00-75.00; 2. "School Children," blue milkglass $70.00-75.00.

Bottom Row: ★Heisey Child's Mug, crystal $400.00-450.00.

★Reproduced in colors.

Banana Stands

Left to Right: 1. Palm Leaf Fan $35.00-45.00; 2. Palm Leaf Fan $35.00-45.00; 3. Beautiful Lady $35.00-45.00; 4. Daisy and Star $35.00-45.00.

Banana Stands

Left to Right: 1. Unknown $35.00-45.00; 2. Fine Cut and Fan $35.00-45.00; 3. Little Ladders $35.00-45.00; 4. Unknown $35.00-45.00.

Cakestands

Front: 1. Rexford, 3¼" $20.00-25.00; 2. Rexford, 3½" $20.00-25.00.
Rear: 1. Ribbon Candy, 3-3/8" $25.00-30.00; 2. Ribbon Candy, 3-3/8" $50.00-55.00; 3. Unknown, 3-1/8" $30.00-35.00.

Cakestands

Front: 1. Roses, 3-3/8" $22.00-25.00; 2. Peacock Feather, 2" $75.00-80.00; 3. Little Ladders, 3¼" $25.00-30.00.
Rear: 1. Unknown, 4" $35.00-40.00. 2. Arrowhead and Oval, 3-5/8" $25.00-30.00.

Cakestands

Front: Thumbprint and Panels, 1″ $25.00-30.00.
Center: 1. Swirl, 2″ $30.00-35.00; 2. "Inverted Swirl,", 2″ $30.00-35.00.
Rear: 1. "Twin Candy," 3-3/8″ $25.00-30.00; 2. Baby Thumbprint, 3″ $75.00-80.00.

Cakestands

Front: Candlewick small comport, 3-1/8″ $15.00-18.00.
Center: 1. "Buttons and Loops," 3-5/8″ $35.00-40.00; 2. Unknown, 4″ $25.00-30.00.
Rear: 1. Beautiful Lady, 3½″ $25.00-30.00; 2. Beautiful Lady, 3-3/8″ $25.00-30.00.

Cakestands

Front: 1. Thumbprint Variation $45.00-50.00; 2. "Flower with Band," $40.00-45.00.
Rear: 1. Palm Leaf Fan $30.00-35.00; 2. Palm Leaf Fan $30.00-35.00; 3. Palm Leaf Fan $30.00-35.00.

Candlesticks

Top Row: ★Three-branch candles, 4-3/8″, all colors $50.00-55.00.
Center Row: ★★Swirl (French), tall, 3-5/8″, amber $28.00-30.00; white milk glass $18.00-20.00; green milk glass $35.00-40.00; blue milk glass $30.00-35.00. Swirl Chamberstick (French), 1-7/8″ short; amber $25.00-30.00; white milk glass $18.00-20.00; blue milk glass $27.00-30.00.
Bottom Row: 1. Fluted chamberstick, 2″, cobalt $75.00-85.00; 2. ★★★Heisey, 2″ $20.00-25.00; 3. & 4. Chamberstick, 2-1/8″, blue, green $35.00-40.00; 5. "Banded Swirl," 2″, white $32.00-35.00; 6. "Banded Swirl," 2″, clear $4.00-5.00.

★Three-branch candle reproduced in crystal, amberina, vaseline, Mother of Pearl, and cobalt. ★★Swirl (French), reproduced in crystal.
★★★Heisey, 2″, reproduced in crystal.

Candlesticks

Top Row: 1. Crystal, 4¼", $30.00-35.00; 2. "Fine Rib," 4", crystal $35.00-45.00; 3. Wild Rose, 4¼", crystal $75.00-80.00; 4. Westmoreland, 4¼", crystal $40.00-42.00; 5. Crystal, 4¾" $40.00-42.00.
Center Row: 1. Column, 4¾" $50.00-55.00; 2. Cobalt, 4" $40.00-45.00; 3. Peach, 4" $35.00-40.00; 4. Crystal, 4¼" $35.00-40.00.
Bottom Row: 1. Crystal (French), 2½" $22.00-25.00; 2. Cambridge, 5/8", green $20.00-22.00; 3. Cambridge, 5/8", blue $15.00-18.00; 4. Crystal, 2" $27.00-30.00.

Candlesticks, Castor Sets, and Miniatures

Top Row: Candles, 2-1/8" yellow, green $125.00-135.00 pair; blue $150.00-155.00 pair. Castor Sets: Left, 2" $60.00-65.00; Center, 2½" $70.00-75.00; Right, 2" $60.00-65.00.
Center Row: Candles, 1-1/8", crystal $45.00-50.00 pair. Cased, colored bases $90.00-100.00 pair.
Bottom Row: 1. Miniature Comport, 2½" $45.00-50.00; 2. Miniature Plate, 2½" $34.00-36.00; 3. Heart and Thumbprint Cake Plate, 1-5/8" $145.00-155.00.

Candlesticks

Top Row: 1. Three-branch, 4¼", crystal $45.00-50.00; 2. Etched, 4-1/8", crystal $35.00-40.00; 3. "Lacy and Beads," 2", cobalt $75.00-80.00; 4. Crystal, 5/8", $12.00-15.00; 5. Heisey, 4½", crystal $20.00-25.00.

Center Row: 1. Crystal, 3¾" $12.00-15.00; 2. *Crystal, 3" $20.00-22.00; 3. Crystal, 5/8" $12.00-15.00; 4. Heisey, 3", crystal $32.00-35.00; 5. **Heisey, 3½", crystal $30.00-32.00.

Bottom Row: 1. "Dutch Kinder," 3", blue milk glass $110.00-125.00; 2. Westmoreland, 2½", crystal $20.00-22.00; 3. Crystal, 2½", $20.00-22.00; 4. "Dutch Kinder," 3", white milk glass $75.00-80.00.

*Reproduced in crystal
**Heisey, 3½", reproduced in crystal, green

Pewter Castor Sets

Top Row: 1. "Banded Ring" $60.00-65.00; 2. "Shield" $85.00-90.00; 3. "Eagle in Circle" $95.00-100.00; 4. "Girl in Hoop" $95.00-100.00.
Center Row: 1. "Star" (dated 1876) $90.00-95.00; 2. Resting Eagle $80.00-85.00; 3. "Fancy Ring" $70.00-75.00.
Bottom Row: 1. "Fancy Wreath" $95.00-100.00; 2. Angel in Ring $95.00-100.00.

Condiment Sets

Left: Hickman: Vinegar Cruet, 3″; Pepper, 3½″; Salt, 1″; Tray, 3¼″x5″. Set $70.00-75.00.
Left Center: Unknown, blue milk glass: Pepper, 3¼″; Salt, 2½″; Tray, 3-1/8″x4¼″. Set $42.00-47.00.
Right Center: Planet: Vinegar Cruet, 3″; Pepper, 3¼″; Salt, 1″; Tray, 2½″x6″. Set $90.00-100.00.
Right: English Hobnail: Vinegar Cruet, 2-7/8″; Pepper, 3¼″; Salt, 7/8″; Tray, 5″. Set $70.00-75.00.

Decanter Set (Bohemian)

The original decanter stopper is also red. Decanter Set, 5 piece $125.00-140.00.

Decanter Set

This "Toy Liquor Set" was authenticated in a 1910 Butler Brother's Catalogue. Gold trim, add 25%.

Decanter, 8¼"	48.00-50.00
Tumbler, 1-7/8"	6.00- 8.00
Set, 5 Piece	72.00-82.00

Enameled Miniatures

Left: Decanter, 5-5/8"; Goblet, 2¼"; Tray, 5¾". Set, 6 piece $135.00-150.00.
Center: Pitcher, 2¾"; Tumbler; Tray, 4-7/8". Set 6 piece $140.00-160.00. Honey Dish (raised inner rim), 1-7/8" $75.00-85.00.
Right: Decanter, 3-1/8" $55.00-65.00; Biscuit Jar, 2-1/8" $45.00-50.00.

Enameled Lemonade Sets

A lemonade set similar to these was advertised in a 1910 Butler Brother's catalogue. The seven piece set sold for 35 cents.

Left: Pitcher, 4¾" $85.00-90.00. Honey Dish, 3¾".
Center: "Lily of the Valley" Pitcher, 5¼" $85.00-95.00; Tumbler, 2¼" $20.00-25.00; Set, 7 piece $205.00-245.00.
Right: "Strawberry" Pitcher, 5-7/8" $85.00-95.00; Crystal Enameled Tumblers $20.00-25.00.

Green Enameled Sets, add 20%.

Tumble Ups

1. Enamel with Vertical Ribs, 3″ $70.00-80.00; 2. Red Bohemian, 3-1/8″ $125.00-145.00; 3. Pink Swirl, 3½″ $175.00-195.00; 4. Green, 4-1/8″ $55.00-65.00; 5. Cut Glass, 2-5/8″ $95.00-125.00.

Miniature Vases
These small vases were made by Sowerby's Elison Glassworks, Ltd., England. They were found in an 1852 catalogue.

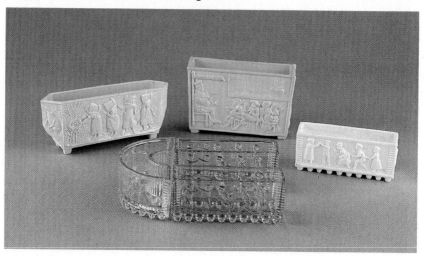

Front: "London Bridge," crystal, rectangular, 1-3/8″x4½″ $60.00-65.00; "London Bridge," crystal, ½ round, 1-3/8″x4½″ $60.00-65.00.
Rear: "London Bridge," white milk glass, 1-3/8″x4½″ $75.00-80.00; "Old King Cole," blue milk glass, 1-5/8″x5″ $95.00-100.00; "Sunbonnet Babies," blue milk glass, hexagonal, 1-3/8″x6¼″ $95.00-100.00.

Cut Glass Miniatures

1. Tumble-up, 2-5/8" $95.00-125.00; 2. Cut Nappy, 3¾" $50.00-60.00; 3. Honey Dish, 2½" $75.00-80.00; 4. Cut Nappy, 4" $50.00-60.00; 5. Vase, 3-3/8" $75.00-80.00.

Sandwich Miniatures
The pieces pictured above range in size from 1¼" to 2-1/8". See page 43

Top Row: 1. Panelled Pitcher and Bowl $200.00-220.00. 2. Panelled Footed Tumbler $45.00-55.00. 3. Panelled Covered Dish $120.00-130.00. 4. Lacy Tureen and Underplate $260.00-280.00. 5. Lacy Compote $190.00-210.00. 6. Panelled Footed Goblet $35.00-45.00. 7. Panelled Bowl and Pitcher $240.00-260.00.
Center Row: 1. *Lacy Creamer $90.00-100.00. 2. Panelled Plate $80.00-90.00. 3. Panelled Underplate $90.00-100.00. 4, 5, & 6. Lacy Plates $80.00-90.00. 7. Lacy "Hearts and Arrows" Plate $120.00-130.00. 8. Lacy Creamer $90.00-100.00.
Center Front: Iron $140.00-160.00.
Bottom Row: 1. Lacy Footed Bowl $90.00-100.00. 2. *Lacy and Scalloped Bowl $115.00-125.00. 3. Lacy Oval Dish $115.00-125.00. 4. Panelled Cup and Saucer $130.00-140.00.

*Reproduced, signed MMA (Metropolitan Museum of Art)

Miscellaneous Miniatures

Top Row: 1. Swirl Creamer $50.00-55.00. 2. Swirl Butter $55.00-60.00. 3. Swirl Sugar and Lid $45.00-50.00. 4. Swirl Creamer, $40.00-45.00. 5. Swirl Compote $45.00-50.00. 6. Swirl Chamberpot $30.00-35.00. 7. Swirl Chamberstick $12.00-14.00.

Center Row: 1. "Star" Butterdish $65.00-70.00. 2. Butterdish $30.00-35.00. 3. Blue Butterdish $55.00-60.00. 4. Butterdish $40.00-45.00. 5. Covered Dish $30.00-35.00. 6. Honey Dish $35.00-40.00. 7. Covered Rectangular Dish $18.00-20.00.

Bottom Row: 1. Buzz Saw Jug $35.00-40.00. 2. D&M No. 42 Rose Bowl $62.00-67.00. 3, 4, & 5. Fenton Vases $22.00-25.00. 6. Swirl Mug $4.00-6.00. 7. Rose Bowl $50.00-60.00.

Miscellaneous
The Wedgewood-type pieces are marked "Made in Germany."

Syrup	40.00-45.00
Planter, 2¾"	65.00-75.00
Biscuit Jar, 3¾"	75.00-80.00

92

Spice Sets

Tall Spice, 6½″	50.00-55.00
Medium Spice, 3½″	20.00-25.00
Short Spice, 2″	4.00- 5.00

Ice Cream Maker

Cone Holder	40.00- 45.00
Ice Tongs, 6″	30.00- 35.00
Ice Cream Freezer, 7½″	95.00-125.00

Fish Set (Federal Glass Co.)

Fish Set

Grape Stein Set (Federal Glass Co.)

Stein Set

"Tulip and Honeycomb" (Federal Glass Co.) Table Set

Wabash Toy Sets

"Tulip and Honeycomb" (Federal Glass Co.) Vegetable Set

Vegetable Set

95

Full-Size Children's Dishes

Alphabet Series (Hazel Atlas Co.)

Bowl, 5″	3.50-4.50	Tumbler, 4¾″	7.00-8.00
Mug, 2-7/8″	3.50-4.50		

Animals (Hazel Atlas Co.)

Three Little Pigs		**Scottie Dog**	
Bowl, 7¾″	5.00-6.00	Bowl, 5″	4.00-4.50
Bowl, 5¾″	4.00-4.50	Mug, 3″	3.50-4.00
Mug, 3¾″	4.00-4.50		
Mug, 3-1/8″	3.50-4.00	"Bosco" Mug, 3½″	5.00-6.00
Plate, 7″	3.50-4.00		

Circus Scenes (Hazel Atlas Co.)

Bowl, 5"	4.00-5.00	Plate, 8"	4.00-5.00
Bowl, 5"	4.00-4.50	Plate, divided	4.00-4.50
Bowl, 5¾"	4.00-4.50	Plate, flashed	2.50-3.50
Mug, flashed, 3¼"	2.50-3.50	Tumbler, 5"	3.00-3.50

Davy Crockett

Bowl (Fireking)	3.00-3.50	Plate, 7"	6.00-7.50
Mug (Fireking),		Tumbler, 12 oz.	3.50-4.00
3¼"	3.00-3.50	Tumbler, 10 oz.	3.50-4.00
Mug (Hazel Atlas)	4.00-4.50	Tumbler, 8 oz.	3.50-4.00

Hopalong Cassidy (Hazel Atlas Co.)

Mug, 3″	5.50- 6.50	Tumbler, 10 oz.	
Tumbler, 10 oz.	10.00-12.00	(red)	12.00-14.00
Tumbler, 9 oz.	14.00-16.00	Tumbler, 5 oz.	25.00-27.00

Hopalong Cassidy and Other Cowboys

Bowl, 5″	12.00-14.00	Mug (Lone Ranger),	
Mug (Indians), 3″	4.00- 4.50	2¼″	15.00-18.00
Mug (Tex), 3″	3.00- 3.50	Plate, 7″	14.00-16.00

Cowboy Collectables (Hazel Atlas Co.)

Bowl (Cisco Kid), 5"	8.00-10.00	Mug (Ranger Joe), 3"	3.00- 3.50
Bowl (Ranger Joe), 5"	4.00- 4.50	Mug (Wyatt Earp), 3"	8.00-10.00
Bowl (Wyatt Earp), 5"	8.00-10.00	Plate, 7"	8.00-10.00
Bowl, divided, 6-5/8"	7.50- 8.50		

Tumblers (Hazel Atlas Co.)

Top Row: 1. Butcher, Baker, and Candlestick Maker $6.00-8.00. 2. Little Boy Blue $6.00-8.00. 3. Mary Had a Little Lamb $5.00-6.00.
Center Row: 1. Mary Had a Little Lamb $6.00-8.00. 2. Little Red Riding Hood $5.00-6.00.
Bottom Row: 1. Jack and Jill $5.00-6.00. 2. The Old Lady in the Shoe $6.00-8.00. 3. Circus Clowns $5.00-6.00.

The plate and the mug on the top right were made by Anchor Hocking. The bowl in the center right is marked "Fireking." The remainder of the pieces were made by Hazel Atlas.

Bowl (Child's prayer)	2.50- 3.50	Mug (Child's prayer), 3"	3.50- 4.00
Bowl (Bo Peep), 7"	6.00- 7.50	Mug (Bo Peep), 3-1/8"	4.50- 5.50
Bowl (Gulliver), 5"	10.00-12.00	Mug (Robin Hood), 3"	8.00-10.00

Space Scenes (Hazel Atlas Co.)

| Mug (top row), 3" | 4.50-5.50 |
| Mug (bottom row), 3-1/8" | 5.50-6.00 |

Shirley Temple

*Bowl, 6½"	55.00-60.00
*Creamer, 4½"	25.00-27.50
*Mug, 3¾"	45.00-55.00

*Reproduced. A juice tumbler with the Shirley Temple decal is currently being made by the Libbey Glass Co.

Depression Era Cereal Bowls

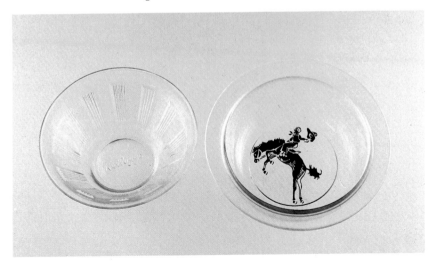

"Kelloggs," pink	25.00-27.00
"Bucking Horse," green	25.00-27.00

Baby Bottles

Baby Bottle	3.00- 4.00
Boxed Set	18.00-23.00
"PET" Measure	12.00-14.00

Baby Reamers

Top Row: White Milk glass with Rabbit $85.00-95.00; Crystal $45.00-50.00.
Center Row: Green $55.00-60.00; Crystal, frosted, Chicks $45.00-50.00; Blue $85.00-90.00.
Bottom Row: Pink $75.00-80.00; Crystal $65.00-70.00; Green $80.00-85.00.

Baby Reamers

Top Row: Green $85.00-90.00; Pink $70.00-80.00; Amber $90.00-100.00.
Center Row: Crystal (left) $32.00-37.00; Crystal (right) $33.00-38.00.
Bottom Row: Crystal, frosted $65.00-70.00.

Part II: China and Pottery

European Sets

Many play sets were made in Germany and England and exported to the United States. Sets were also made in Austria, France, Czechoslavakia, and other countries of Europe.

Although cocoa sets, coffee sets, and dessert sets were made, tea sets and dinner sets are most commonly found. Most European sets consist of a service for six.

The size of the pieces in the set depended on their intended use. Large demitasse-like pieces were used by little girls to have parties with their playmates. Small-size pieces were used for make-believe parties with dolls. Even smaller "miniature" pieces were used to decorate ornate doll houses.

Kitchenware and other accessary items were also made, but these pieces are usually expensive and are not easily found.

Fish Set (Austria)

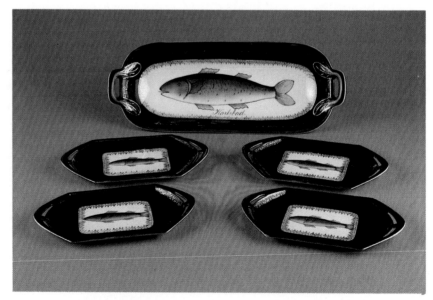

Plate, 6½"	20.00- 22.00
Set, 7 piece	190.00-200.00
Platter, 11¼"	60.00- 70.00

Silhouette Children ("Victoria Czecho-Slovakia")

Creamer, 2-1/8"	5.00- 6.00
Cup, 1-7/8"	3.50- 4.00
Plate	3.00- 3.50
Set, 4 Place	50.00-57.00
Saucer, 3¼"	.75- 1.00
Sugar and Lid	6.00- 7.00
Teapot and Lid, 3-5/8"	14.00-16.00

Roman Chariots ("Cauldon England")

Creamer, 2"	22.00- 27.00
Cup, 1¾"	20.00- 22.50
Saucer	4.00- 5.00
Set, 6 Place	205.00-215.00
Sugar, 1½"	20.00- 25.00
Teapot and Lid, 3-3/8"	50.00- 55.00

Scenes From Chas Dicken's Old Curiosity Shop ("Ridgway's England")

	Dinner Set		**Tea Set**
Casserole	40.00-50.00	Creamer	22.00- 27.00
Gravy Boat, 5½"	25.00-30.00	Cup, 1-5/8"	16.00- 18.00
Plate, 3-7/8"	8.00-10.00	Plate, 4-3/8"	8.00- 10.00
Plate, 4½"	10.00-12.00	Saucer, 4"	2.00- 3.00
Platter, 5"	20.00-25.00	Set, 6 Place	280.00-325.00
Platter, 6"	25.00-30.00	Sugar	18.00- 20.00
Platter, 7"	28.00-32.00	Teapot and Lid,	
Platter, 8"	28.00-32.00	4½"	50.00- 55.00
Soup Bowl	14.00-16.00	Waste Bowl, 1-7/8"	35.00- 40.00
Tureen, 4¾"	40.00-45.00		

Kite Set (England)

Gravy Boat, 3¼"	95.00-100.00	Tureen, 3¼"x4¼"	125.00-150.00
Plate, 3½"	44.00- 48.00	Underplate,	
Plate, 2½"	42.00- 46.00	3½"x5¼"	90.00- 95.00
Plate, 2¾"	44.00- 48.00	Vegetable, covered,	
Soup, 3½"	50.00- 55.00	3½"	95.00-100.00
Tureen, 2½"x3¼"	125.00-150.00		

May (England)
The teapot and the creamer on the right are marked "Staffordshire, England."

	Left Set			**Right Set**	
Creamer	14.00-	16.00	Creamer	15.00-	17.00
Cup, 2-1/8"	12.00-	14.00	Cup, 2-1/8"	12.00-	14.00
Plate, 5-3/8"	6.00-	7.00	Plate, 5-3/8"	6.50-	7.50
Saucer, 4½"	2.00-	3.00	Saucer, 4½"	2.50-	3.50
Sugar and Lid, 4¼"	15.00-	18.00	Sugar and Lid, 4¼"	17.00-	19.00
Teapot and Lid, 5"	34.00-	37.50	Teapot and Lid, 5"	35.00-	38.00
Set, 4 Place	140.00-	165.00	Set, 4 Place	145.00-	170.00

Punch and Judy (England)

Creamer, 3¼"	22.00-	25.00	Sugar and Lid, 4½"	22.00-	25.00
Cup, 1-7/8"	22.00-	25.00	Teapot and Lid, 5"	55.00-	60.00
Plate, 5¾"	18.00-	20.00	Waste Bowl, 2-1/8"	37.00-	40.00
Saucer, 4¼"	10.00-	12.00	Set, 4 Place	330.00-	370.00

Scenes From England

Shown below on the plate and the soup bowl is the DeGout Castle. The vegetable bowl pictures Leclad's Bridge. These pieces are part of a dinner set in which each piece depicts an English scene. Some of the other scenes not shown are Tewkesbury Church, Sysham Monastery, Longington Park, Blaize Castle, and Kenelworth Park.

Plate, 3-1/8″	18.00-20.00
Soup, 3-5/8″	22.00-25.00
Vegetable, covered, 3-7/8″	65.00-75.00

Water Hen (England)

Some pieces of this set are marked "Water Hen, Caason's England." Others bear the mark "Staffordshire, England."

Creamer, 3-1/8″	22.00- 25.00
Cup, 2″	11.00- 13.00
Plate, 5½″	7.00- 8.00
Saucer, 4-3/8″	3.50- 4.50
Sugar and Lid, 4½″	25.00- 27.00
Teapot and Lid, 5¼″	37.50- 40.00
Waste Bowl, 2½″	27.50- 30.00
Set, 4 Place	200.00-225.00

Blue Marble ("England")

Bowl, oval, 4½"	30.00- 35.00	Tureen, 4¼"	40.00- 45.00
Gravy Boat, 1½"	30.00- 35.00	Underplate, 5½"	29.00- 32.00
Plate, 4"	10.00- 12.00	Tureen, 3½"	35.00- 40.00
Platter, 4½"	28.00- 30.00	Underplate, 4½"	28.00- 30.00
Platter, 4½"	28.00- 30.00	Set, 4 Place	300.00-340.00

Pagodas (England)

Casserole, covered,		Platter, 7-1/8"	25.00- 30.00
5½"	40.00- 45.00	Platter, 6-1/8"	25.00- 27.00
Plate, 4½"	9.00- 12.00	Platter, 5-1/8"	20.00- 25.00
Plate, 3-7/8"	8.00- 10.00	Set, 6 Place	180.00-215.00

"Girls With Pets" ("Charles Allerton and Sons, England")

Creamer, 3-1/8"	12.00- 15.00
Cup, 2-1/8"	9.00- 11.00
Plate, 5¼"	6.00- 7.00
Saucer, 4½"	2.00- 3.00
Sugar and Lid, 4½"	15.00- 17.00
Teapot and Lid, '8" 5-1/8"	25.00- 30.00
Set, 4 Place	120.00-145.00

Stick Spatter ("Staffordshire, England")

Creamer, 3-1/8"	30.00- 35.00
Cup, 2"	16.00- 18.00
Plate, 5-3/8"	10.00- 12.00
Saucer, 4½"	3.00- 4.00
Sugar and Lid, 4½"	25.00- 30.00
Teapot and Lid, 5"	50.00- 55.00
Waste Bowl, 2½"	40.00- 45.00
Set, 4 Place	250.00-300.00

Mary Had A Little Lamb ("Brentleigh Ware Staffordshire, England")

Creamer, 1½"	5.00- 6.00
Cup, 1-7/8"	5.00- 6.00
Plate, 3¾"	4.00- 5.00
Saucer, 3-3/8"	1.50- 2.00
Sugar, 1-1/8"	5.00- 6.00
Teapot and Lid, 3½"	25.00-27.00
Set, 4 Place	75.00-80.00

Dessert Set (England)

Comport, 3-1/8"	35.00- 40.00
Plate, 2-handle, 4¼"	25.00- 30.00
Plate, scallopped, 2-handle, 4-5/8"	30.00- 35.00
Set, 6 Place	235.00-265.00
Plate, 4"	20.00- 22.00
Platter, oval, 5"	25.00- 30.00

Maiden-Hair-Fern ("Ridgway's Stoke-on-Trent, England")

Casserole, 5¼"	25.00- 28.00	Soup, 4½"	10.00- 12.00
Underplate, 5"	12.00- 14.00	Tureen, 6-3/8"	32.00- 35.00
Plate, 3-5/8"	5.00- 7.00	Underplate, 6-7/8"	14.00- 16.00
Plate, 4½"	6.00- 8.00	Tureen, 4-1/8"	27.00- 30.00
Platter, 8"	15.00- 18.00	Underplate, 4-5/8"	12.00- 14.00
Platter, 7¼"	13.00- 15.00	Set, 6 Place	280.00-350.00
Platter, 6"	12.00- 14.00		

Gaudy Ironstone (England)

Creamer, 2-3/8"	27.00- 30.00	Teapot and Lid,	
Cup, 1-7/8"	20.00- 22.00	4½"	60.00- 70.00
Platter, 6"	30.00- 35.00	Waste Bowl, 2-7/8"	45.00- 50.00
Saucer	12.00- 15.00	Set, 4 Place	330.00-360.00
Sugar and Lid, 4"	35.00- 40.00		

Sarreguemine

Creamer	30.00- 35.00
Cup, 2-3/16"	20.00- 25.00
Plate, 6"	32.00- 35.00
Saucer, 5-3/8"	8.00- 10.00
Sugar and Lid	40.00- 45.00
Teapot and Lid, 5½"	90.00- 95.00
Set, 4 Place	400.00-450.00

Saint Nicholas (Germany)

Creamer, 3"	27.00- 30.00
Cup, 2-1/8"	18.00- 20.00
Plate, 5-1/8"	12.00- 14.00
Saucer, 4½"	6.00- 8.00
Sugar and Lid, 3"	28.00- 32.00
Teapot and Lid, 5½"	75.00- 85.00
Set, 6 Place	325.00-375.00

Joseph, Mary, and the Donkey (Germany)

Creamer, 3″	25.00- 27.00
★Cup, 2-3/8″	14.00- 16.00
Plate, 7″	7.00- 9.00
Saucer, 4¾″	4.00- 5.00
Sugar and Lid, 3″	22.00- 25.00
Teapot and Lid	65.00- 70.00
Set, 6 Place	265.00-300.00
★Angel in Chariot, right	

Green Luster "Merry Christmas" ("Leuchtenberg, Germany")

Creamer, 2-7/8″	21.00- 23.00
Cup, 2-1/8″	11.00- 12.00
Plate, 5″	6.50- 7.50
Saucer, 4½″	4.00- 5.00
Sugar and Lid, 3-5/8″	21.00- 23.00
Teapot and Lid, 4-7/8″	60.00- 65.00
Set, 6 Place	230.00-250.00

Angel Christmas Set (Germany)

Above are pieces to three different sets with the same type decal. The color of the decal varies, and the shapes of the pieces are slightly different, but the sets are priced about the same.

Creamer, 3-3/8"	22.00- 25.00
Creamer, 3¾"	22.00- 25.00
Cup, 2¼"	14.00- 16.00
Plate, 5-1/8"	7.00- 9.00
Saucer	4.00- 5.00
Sugar and Lid, 4-1/8"	26.00- 28.00
Teapot and Lid, 6½"	55.00- 60.00
Teapot and Lid, 6¼"	55.00- 60.00
Set, 6 Place	330.00-375.00

Pink Luster "Merry Christmas" (Germany)

Creamer, 2-7/8"	23.00- 25.00
Cup, 2-1/8"	13.00- 15.00
Plate, 5"	7.00- 8.00
Saucer, 4½"	4.00- 5.00
Sugar and Lid, 3-5/8"	24.00- 26.00
Teapot and Lid, 4-7/8"	67.00- 70.00
Set, 6 Place	260.00-290.00

Pink Luster Sets (Germany)

Many different decals were often applied to the same blanks. The picture above shows a cup and saucer from a Christmas set, a plate with a hunt scene, and the teapot features a chauffeur-driven car. Although all luster sets are highly desirable, the Christmas set is probably the most prized.

Creamer	20.00-22.00	Saucer	4.00- 5.00
Cup	12.00-14.00	Sugar and Lid	22.00-25.00
Plate	7.00- 8.00	Teapot and Lid	65.00-70.00

Children Luster Sets (Germany)

Similar sets with various decals picturing children are shown. The teapot with the bear is very desirable.

Creamer, 2½"	10.00-12.00	Teapot and Lid,	
Cup, 1-7/8"	6.00- 8.00	5¼"	40.00-50.00
Plate, 5¼"	4.00- 5.00	Teapot and Lid,	
Saucer, 4-1/8"	2.00- 3.00	(Teddy Bear),	
Sugar and Lid, 3½"	8.00-10.00	4½"	55.00-60.00

"Brundage Girls" (Germany)

Creamer, 4"	18.00-20.00
Cup, 1-3/16"	14.00-16.00
Mug, 2¾"	28.00-30.00
Plate, 6¼"	15.00-18.00
Saucer, 4"	4.00- 5.00

"The Bridesmaid" (Germany)

Creamer, 3-3/8"	16.00- 18.00
Cup, 2½"	12.00- 14.00
Plate	6.00- 8.00
Saucer, 4-7/8"	4.00- 5.00
Sugar and Lid, 3"	20.00- 25.00
Teapot and Lid, 5½"	50.00- 55.00
Mug, 2-5/8"	18.00- 20.00
Set, 6 Place	220.00-260.00

"Buster Brown" (Germany)

Creamer, 2-7/8"	30.00- 35.00
Cup, 2½"	30.00- 35.00
Plate, 5"	28.00- 30.00
Saucer, 4-5/8"	9.00- 12.00
Sugar and Lid, 3¾"	55.00- 65.00
Teapot and Lid, 5-7/8"	140.00-160.00
Set, 6 Place	500.00-600.00

"The House That Jack Built" (Germany)

Creamer, 3-3/8"	15.00- 17.00
Cup, 1-7/8"	10.00- 12.00
Plate, 5¼"	5.00- 6.00
Saucer, 4"	3.00- 4.00
Sugar and Lid, 3½"	15.00- 17.00
Teapot and Lid, 5¾"	40.00- 45.00
Set, 6 Place	175.00-200.00

Nursery Rhyme Set (Germany)

Creamer, 1-7/8"	9.00- 11.00
Cup, 1¾"	7.00- 8.00
Plate	4.00- 5.00
Saucer, 3¾"	2.50- 3.50
Sugar, 1-3/8"	9.00- 11.00
Teapot and Lid	27.50- 30.00
Set, 6 Place	125.00-150.00

Nursery Scenes (Germany)

Creamer, 3"	10.00- 12.00
Cup, 2"	7.00- 8.00
Plate	4.00- 4.50
Saucer	2.00- 3.00
Sugar and Lid, 3¼"	12.00- 14.00
Teapot and Lid, 4½"	30.00- 32.50
Set, 6 Place	130.00-150.00

Blue Portrait (Germany)

Creamer, 2¾"	20.00- 25.00
Cup, 1-5/8"	16.00- 18.00
Plate, 3½"	8.00- 10.00
Saucer, 3¼"	4.00- 5.00
Sugar and Lid, 2-7/8"	20.00- 25.00
Teapot and Lid, 4½"	55.00- 65.00
Tray, 5"	25.00- 27.00
Set, 4 Place	235.00-275.00

Coffee Set (Germany)

Coffee pot, 6"	15.00-18.00
Creamer, 2-3/8"	6.00- 8.00
Cup, 2-1/8"	5.00- 6.00
Plate, 5¼"	3.00- 4.00
Saucer, 4"	2.00- 3.00
Sugar and Lid, 3¾"	6.00- 8.00
Set, 4 Place	70.00-85.00

Floral Tea Set (Germany)

Creamer	8.00- 10.00	Sugar and Lid	8.00- 10.00
Cup	7.00- 8.00	Teapot and Lid	20.00- 25.00
Plate	4.00- 5.00	Set, 6 Place	120.00-140.00
Saucer	2.00- 3.00		

Floral Set (Germany)

Creamer	12.00- 14.00	Sugar and Lid, 3½"	15.00- 18.00
Cup, 2-3/16"	9.00- 11.00	Teapot and Lid,	
Plate	5.00- 6.00	5¼"	40.00- 45.00
Saucer, 4-3/8"	3.50- 4.50	Set, 6 Place	170.00-200.00

Floral Sets (Germany)

	Pink	Blue
Creamer	3.00- 4.00	4.00- 4.50
Cup	3.00- 3.50	3.50- 4.00
Plate	2.00- 2.50	2.50- 3.00
Saucer	1.00- 1.25	1.50- 2.00
Sugar and Lid	4.00- 5.00	4.50- 5.50
Teapot and Lid	10.00-12.00	14.00-16.00
Set, 6 Place	55.00-65.00	65.00-80.00

Floral Cabaret Set (Dresden)

Creamer, 2½"	27.00- 29.00
Cup, 2-1/8"	22.00- 24.00
Saucer, 4"	10.00- 12.00
Sugar and Lid, 3"	30.00- 32.00
Teapot and Lid, 4¾"	80.00- 85.00
Tray, 8¼"x9-5/8"	25.00- 30.00
Set, 2 Place	235.00-250.00

Cabaret Sets (Germany)

	White/Blue	Pink/Gold
Creamer	10.00-12.00	14.00- 16.00
Cup	7.00- 8.00	12.00- 14.00
Saucer	2.50- 3.00	4.00- 5.00
Sugar and Lid	12.00-14.00	17.00- 18.00
Teapot and Lid	22.00-25.00	50.00- 55.00
Tray	9.00-11.00	14.00- 16.00
Set, 2 Place	80.00-90.00	130.00-145.00

Stein Set ("Bavaria")

Stein (Character), 1-7/8″	8.00- 9.00
Stein (Shield), 1-7/8″	3.00- 4.00
Tray, 5¾″x7-7/8″	15.00-17.00

Blue Onion Kitchenware (Germany)

Box, Mehl, 4¼"	100.00-125.00
Box, Salt, 4¼"	100.00-125.00
Egg Whip, 4½"	60.00- 70.00
Meat Tenderizer, 7"	80.00- 90.00
Rolling Pin, 8"	150.00-175.00
Spoon, 5½"	50.00- 60.00

Figural Spice Set ("Germany")

Cannister, 2½"	28.00-32.00
Cannister, 3¾"	34.00-36.00
Oil, Vinegar, 3½"	35.00-45.00
Salt Box, 3¼"	55.00-60.00

Blue Banded Spice Set ("Germany")

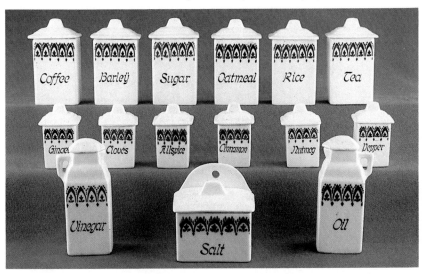

Cannister, 2½"	14.00- 16.00	Vinegar, Oil, 4¼"	20.00- 25.00
Cannister, 3-5/8"	17.00- 19.00	Set, 15 Piece	255.00-295.00
Salt Box, 3-1/8"	30.00- 35.00		

Floral Spice Set (Germany)

Although the cannisters in the bottom row are the same size and shape as those pictured above them, their floral design is slightly different. They are part of a different set, but are so similar that they have been priced together.

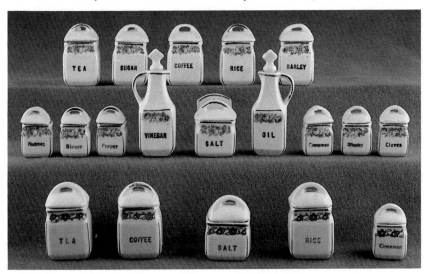

Cannister, 2-1/8"	10.00-12.00	Oil, Vinegar, 3-3/8"	20.00-25.00
Cannister, 1¾"	6.00- 8.00	Salt Box, 1-7/8"	27.00-30.00

125

Spice Sets (Germany and Japan)

Both of these sets are from the same size mold. The set on the left is marked "Germany." The crude irridized floral set on the right was made in Japan.

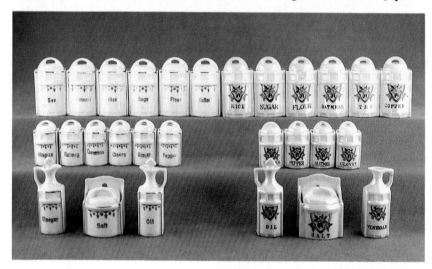

	Germany	**Japan**
Cannister, 2¼"	9.00-11.00	6.00- 8.00
Cannister, 3¼"	12.00-14.00	8.00-10.00
Oil, Vinegar, 3¾"	15.00-17.00	10.00-12.00
Salt Box, 2¾"	22.00-27.00	13.00-15.00

Japan and Occupied Japan Sets

Imports of Japanese children's dishes flourished between World War I and World War II. During World War II this supply was interrupted. After the war, the flood of cheap imports resumed and American-made and European products suffered severely. Between the end of World War II and April 28, 1952, the period of the American occupation, many sets were marked "Occupied Japan." Although most of these sets lack the quality of European sets, they are highly collectible by those interested in "Occupied Japan" items.

Sets may be found boxed in any number of combinations. Two, three, and four place tea sets are most common. Matching dinner sets may be found in many patterns to accompany the tea sets.

Floral Set ("Nippon")

Creamer, 2¼ "	6.00- 7.00
Cup, 1½ "	4.00- 5.00
Plate, 5 "	3.00- 4.00
Saucer, 4¼ "	2.00- 3.00
Sugar and Lid, 3 "	7.00- 9.00
Teapot and Lid, 3¼ "	12.00-14.00
Set, 4 Place	70.00-80.00

Floral Dinner Set ("Made in Japan")

Casserole, 6-5/8″	10.00-12.00	Sugar and Lid,	
Creamer, 2-1/8″	4.00- 4.50	3-5/8″	5.00- 6.00
Cup, 1-5/8″	3.00- 4.00	Teapot and Lid,	
Plate, 5″	2.00- 2.50	3½″	12.00-14.00
Saucer, 4-3/8″	1.00- 1.50	Set, 4 Place	65.00-80.00
Tureen, 5½″	9.00-11.00		

Otter Cocoa Set ("Noritake")

Creamer, 2″	40.00- 45.00	Sugar and Lid	45.00- 50.00
Cup, 1-5/8″	25.00- 27.00	Teapot and Lid	95.00-110.00
Plate, 4¼″	13.00- 15.00	Set, 4 Place	355.00-395.00
Saucer, 3¾″	5.00- 6.00		

Silhouette ("Noritake")

Cup, 1¼"	7.00- 8.00
Plate, 4¼"	4.00- 5.00
Saucer, 3¾"	2.00- 3.00
Teapot and Lid, 3½"	35.00-40.00

Bluebird Dinner Set ("Noritake")

Casserole, 6"	35.00- 40.00	Platter, 7-1/8"	12.00- 14.00
Creamer, 1-7/8"	12.00- 15.00	Saucer, 3¾"	2.00- 3.00
Cup, 1¼"	6.00- 7.00	Sugar and Lid, 2¾"	15.00- 18.00
Plate, 4¼"	4.00- 5.00	Teapot and Lid,	
Set, 4 Place	160.00-190.00	3½"	35.00- 40.00

Floral Dinner Set ("Noritake--Made In Japan")

Casserole, covered, 6"	10.00-12.00	Platter, 7-1/8"	9.00-10.00
Creamer, 1-7/8"	7.00- 9.00	Saucer, 3¾"	2.00- 3.00
Cup, 1-3/8"	5.00- 6.00	Sugar and Lid, 2-7/8"	8.00-10.00
Plate, 4¼"	3.00- 4.00	Set, 4 Place	85.00-90.00

Sunset ("Made in Japan")

Creamer, 1-7/8"	3.00- 4.00	Sugar and Lid, 3-1/8"	4.00- 5.00
Cup, 1¼"	2.00- 3.00	Teapot and Lid, 3¾"	6.00- 7.00
Plate, 4¼"	1.50- 2.00		
Saucer, 3-3/8"	1.00- 1.50		
Set, 4 Place	38.00-42.00		

Chinaman Set (Japan)

Creamer, 2-3/16″	25.00- 27.00
Cup, 1-1/8″	14.00- 16.00
Saucer, 2-7/8″	4.00- 5.00
Sugar and Lid, 2-7/8″	35.00- 37.00
Teapot and Lid, 3-5/8″	45.00- 50.00
Set, 4 Place	175.00-200.00

Silhouette ("Made in Japan")

Cup, 1½″	4.00-5.00
Platter, 6″	6.00-7.00
Saucer, 3¾″	2.00-2.50
Teapot and Lid, 4-1/8″	7.00-8.00

Blue Willow and Red Willow ("Made in Japan")

Blue Willow is found in a variety of sizes. The photograph below shows a large-size Blue Willow dinner set. Included are the hard-to-find napkins, grill plates, 5″ dinner plates, soup bowls and oval vegetable bowl.

The photo on page 133 includes pieces from a small-size Blue Willow dinner set and a small-size Red Willow tea set. Red Willow child's pieces are unusual.

An example of miniature Blue Willow may be found on page 143.

Large Blue Willow Dinner Set

Bowl, 3½″	12.00-14.00
Bowl, oval, 5-3/8″	12.00-15.00
Cakeplate, 5¼″	12.00-14.00
Casserole, 5½″	16.00-18.00
Casserole, 5″	15.00-18.00
Creamer, 2″	7.00- 8.00
Cup, 1½″	5.00- 6.00
Gravy Boat	18.00-20.00
Grill Plate, 5″	18.00-20.00
Grill Plate, 4¼″	17.00-19.00
Knife, 4½″	12.00-15.00
Napkins	8.00-12.00
Plate, 5″	14.00-16.00
Plate, 4-3/8″	8.00-10.00
Platter, 6″	7.00- 9.00
Saucer, 3¾″	1.50- 2.00
Sugar and Lid, 2¾″	7.00-10.00
Teapot and Lid, 3¾″	35.00-40.00
Tureen, 4½″	15.00-18.00
Tureen, 4″	15.00-18.00

Small-Size Blue Willow Dinner Set and Red Willow Tea Set

	Small-Size Blue Willow	Small-Size Red Willow
Creamer, 1½″	7.00- 8.00	15.00-17.00
Cup, 1-1/8″	5.00- 6.00	9.00-10.00
Plate, 3¾″	3.00- 4.00	6.00- 7.00
Platter, 4-5/8″	8.00-10.00	
Saucer, 3-3/8″	1.50- 2.00	3.00- 4.00
Casserole, 4¾″	15.00-18.00	
Underplate, 4-5/8″	6.00- 7.00	
Sugar and Lid, 2″	7.00- 9.00	15.00-17.00
Teapot and Lid, 2-5/8″	35.00-45.00	45.00-50.00

Bears ("Made in Japan")

The cup and saucer on the right was made in England. The cup and saucer in the foreground has "JOSEPH HORNE CO. TOY STORE" on the back of the cup.

Casserole, covered, 2¼″	12.00-15.00	Saucer, 4¼″	3.00- 4.00
		Saucer, 3-5/8″	3.00- 4.00
Cup, 2-3/16″	11.00-13.00	Sugar and Lid	12.00-14.00
Cup, 1-9/16″	11.00-12.00	Cup (England), 1¾″	12.00-14.00
Creamer, 2½″	10.00-12.00	Saucer (England), 4″	4.00- 5.00
Plate, 5″	5.00- 6.00		
Platter, 6¼″	4.00- 6.00		

Mickey Mouse and Little Orphan Annie ("Made In Japan")

Mickey Mouse

Creamer, 2"	7.50- 8.00
Cup, 1-3/16"	5.00- 6.00
Plate, 3¼"	4.00- 5.00
Saucer, 3¼"	1.50- 2.00
Sugar and Lid, 2¾"	8.50-10.00
Teapot and Lid, 3¾"	18.00-20.00
Set, 4 Place	75.00-90.00

Little Orphan Annie

Plate, 4¼"	6.00- 7.00
Platter, 5"	10.00-12.00
Saucer, 3¾"	2.00- 3.00
Tureen, 4½"	16.00-18.00

Mickey Mouse and Peter Pan

This Mickey Mouse set, which differs slightly in style from the one in the top photo, is marked "Occupied Japan."

Mickey Mouse

Cup, 1-3/16"	7.00- 8.00
Plate, 3¾"	6.00- 7.00
Saucer, 3-3/8"	2.00- 3.00
Sugar and Lid, 2¼"	11.00-12.00
Teapot and Lid, 3¼"	25.00-27.00

Peter Pan

Cup, 1-3/16"	5.00- 5.50
Plate, 3-7/8"	3.50- 4.00
Saucer, 3½"	1.50- 2.00

Snow White ("© 1937, W.D. Ent. Made In Japan")

Creamer, 2″	5.00- 6.00
Cup, 1½″	4.50- 5.00
Plate, 4-3/8″	3.50- 4.00
Saucer, 2¾″	1.00- 1.50
Sugar and Lid, 2-3/8″	7.00- 9.00
Teapot and Lid, 3¼″	20.00-22.00
Set, 4 Place	70.00-80.00

Clown, With Duck and Dog on Ball ("Made In Japan")

Creamer, 1¾″	4.00- 4.50
Cup, 1-1/8″	3.50- 4.00
Plate, 3¾″	3.00- 3.50
Saucer, 3-3/8″	1.00- 1.50
Sugar and Lid, 2-5/8″	4.50- 5.00
Teapot and Lid, 3¾″	10.00-12.00
Tray, 4¼″	4.50- 5.00
Set, 4 Place	53.00-63.00

Elephant Luster Set ("Made in Japan")

Creamer, 2"	8.00-10.00	Teapot and Lid,	
Cup, 7/8"	2.00- 2.50	3¼"	15.00-17.00
Saucer, 2¾"	1.00- 1.50	Set, 4 Place	50.00-55.00
Sugar and Lid,			
2-3/8"	10.00-12.00	Without luster, 50% less	

Tan Luster Floral Utility Set ("Made In Japan")

Bowl, covered,		Platter, 3-3/8"	3.00- 4.00
1-5/8"	6.00- 8.00	Reamer, 2-5/8"	60.00-65.00
Casserole, oval,		Salt and Pepper,	
1-5/8"	8.00-10.00	1¼"	10.00-12.00
Casserole, round,		Salt Box, 2-1/8"	15.00-18.00
1½"	8.00-10.00	Spatula	5.00- 7.00
Cakeplate, 3¾"	8.00-10.00	Teapot and Lid, 3"	10.00-12.00
Creamer, 1½"	4.00- 5.00	Teapot and Lid, 2"	10.00-12.00
Ice Bucket, 2-1/8"	8.00-10.00	Waffle Dish, 1½"	14.00-16.00
Platter, 3-7/8"	3.00- 4.00		

Dutch Children ("Made In Japan")

Creamer	3.00- 4.00
Cup	2.50- 3.00
Plate	2.00- 3.00
Saucer	1.50- 2.00
Sugar and Lid	4.00- 5.00
Teapot and Lid	8.00-10.00
Set, 4 Place	40.00-50.00

Tan and Grey Luster ("Phoenix China Made In Japan")

Creamer, 2¼"	7.00- 8.00
Cup, 1½"	4.00- 5.00
Plate, 3"	3.00- 4.00
Saucer, 2¾"	1.00- 1.25
Sugar and Lid, 2-5/8"	7.00- 8.00
Teapot and Lid, 4"	18.00-20.00
Set, 4 Place	65.00-75.00

Floral Decorated Sets ("Made In Japan")

Cakeplate, 6″	2.50- 3.00	Sugar and Lid, 2½″	2.50- 3.00
Creamer, 2″	3.00- 4.00	Teapot and Lid,	
Cup, 1-1/8″	1.50- 2.00	3-5/8″	4.00- 5.00
Plate, 3-5/8″	1.00- 1.50	Set, 4 Place	25.00-30.00
Saucer, 4¾″	1.00- 1.25		

Floral Boxed Cake Set (Japan)

Cakeplate, 4-3/8″	3.50- 4.00	Sugar and Lid,	
Creamer, 2¼″	3.00- 3.50	2-5/8″	3.50- 4.00
Cup, 1-1/8″	1.50- 2.00	Teapot and Lid,	
Plate, 3¾″	1.50- 2.00	3-5/8″	5.00- 6.00
Saucer, 3¼″	1.00- 1.25	Set, 4 Place	32.00-37.00

Floral Boxed Set (Japan)

Creamer, 1-3/8″	3.00- 4.00
Cup, 7/8″	2.00- 2.50
Saucer, 3¼″	1.00- 1.50
Sugar and Lid, 2-1/8″	4.00- 5.00
Teapot and Lid, 2-5/8″	8.00- 9.00
Set, 2 Place	20.00-25.00

Butterfly Set ("Made In Japan")

Creamer, 2¼″	4.00- 5.00
Cup, 1½″	2.50- 3.00
Plate, 4-7/8″	2.00- 2.50
Saucer, 4-1/8″	1.00- 1.50
Sugar and Lid, 3-1/8″	4.50- 5.00
Teapot and Lid, 3-3/8″	7.00- 8.00
Set, 4 Place	40.00-45.00

Bluebirds, Geisha, and Dutch Children (Japan)

Creamer, 2"	4.00- 5.00
Cup, 1-1/8"	2.50- 3.00
Plate, 3-5/8"	2.00- 2.50
Saucer, 3¼"	1.00- 1.50
Sugar and Lid, 2¼"	4.00- 5.00
*Teapot and Lid, 3¼"	7.00- 8.00
Set, 4 Place	40.00-45.00

*Geisha, $22.00-25.00

Dutch Figures and Floral Set (Japan)

	Dutch Figures	Floral
Creamer	3.00- 4.00	2.00- 3.00
Cup	2.00- 3.00	2.00- 2.50
Plate	1.00- 1.50	1.00- 1.50
Saucer	1.00- 1.50	1.00- 1.25
Sugar and Lid	3.00- 4.00	2.00- 3.00
Teapot and Lid	5.00- 6.00	4.00- 5.00
Set, 4 Place	34.00-38.00	28.00-32.00

Floral Medallion ("Made In Japan")

Creamer, 2¾ ″	2.00- 2.50	Sugar and Lid, 2½ ″	2.00- 2.50
Cup, 1¾ ″	1.50- 2.00	Teapot and Lid,	
Plate, 4¼ ″	1.00- 1.50	3¾ ″	3.00- 4.00
Saucer, 3-1/8 ″	1.00- 1.25	Set, 4 Place	24.00-28.00

Dinner Sets ("Made In Japan")

Casserole	3.00- 4.00	Salt and Pepper	2.00- 3.00
Creamer	2.00- 2.50	Sugar and Lid	2.00- 3.00
Cup	1.00- 1.50	Teapot and Lid	4.00- 5.00
Plate	1.00- 1.50	Tureen	3.00- 4.00
Platter	2.00- 3.00	Set, 4 Place	35.00-40.00
Saucer	1.00- 1.25		

Mieto ("Hand Painted Made In Japan")

Creamer, 1-7/8″	2.00- 3.00
Cup, 1-15/16″	2.00- 2.50
Plate, 4¾″	1.00- 1.25
Saucer, 3-7/8″	.75- 1.00
Sugar and Lid, 2½″	3.00- 4.00
Teapot and Lid, 3″	6.00- 7.00
Set, 4 Place	30.00-35.00

Ballerina ("© General Ind. NY Japan")

Creamer, 2-5/8″	3.00- 3.50
Cup, 1½″	2.00- 3.00
Plate, 4½″	1.00- 1.50
Saucer, 3-1/8″	1.00- 1.25
Sugar and Lid, 3-3/8″	3.50- 4.00
Teapot and Lid	6.00- 7.00
Set, 4 Place	30.00-35.00

Occupied Japan Sets

The small white set shown in the right foreground is not marked. The set came in a match box-type box which was marked "Occupied Japan."

	Blue Willow	Floral Set	Tan Luster
Casserole	18.00-20.00		
Creamer	8.00-10.00	4.00- 5.00	4.00- 5.00
Cup	6.00- 7.00	3.00- 3.50	3.00- 3.50
Platter	13.00-14.00		
Plate	4.00- 4.50	2.00- 3.00	
Sugar and Lid	10.00-12.00	5.00- 6.00	5.00- 6.00
Teapot and Lid		8.00- 9.00	7.50- 9.00
Tureen	20.00-22.00		

Occupied Japan Sets

Although the set in the box is only marked "Made in Japan," the box is marked "Occupied Japan."

	Blue Willow	Boxed Set	White Floral Set
Cup	4.00- 5.00	3.00- 4.00	3.00- 3.50
Creamer	5.00- 5.50	4.00- 4.50	4.00- 4.50
Saucer	2.50- 3.00	2.00- 2.50	1.50- 2.00
Sugar and Lid	5.50- 6.50	4.00- 5.00	4.50- 5.00
Teapot and Lid	9.00-11.00	7.00- 9.00	6.00- 8.00
Tray			4.00- 5.00

American Made Tea Sets

Several American china and pottery companies made miniature versions of their adult dishes for children. The pieces were large enough for children to use to give tea parties for their playmates. Production of these sets peaked during World War II when cheaper Japanese imports were not available. After the war, production declined and many of the companies folded. Today, American made sets are not extremely expensive, although they are not easily found.

Kate Greenaway ("Cleve-ron China U.S.A ")

Cup, 2-1/8"	18.00- 20.00	Sugar and Lid, 3-1/8"	25.00- 27.00
Creamer, 2½"	22.00- 25.00	Teapot and Lid, 3½"	55.00- 60.00
Plate, 6"	12.00- 14.00		
Saucer, 4½"	5.00- 6.00		
Tray, 7¼"	20.00- 25.00	Set, 4 Place	275.00-300.00

Cameoware (Harker)

Cup, 2¼"	5.00-6.00	Saucer, 4-7/8"	2.00-2.50
Plate, 7¼"	6.00-7.00		

Circus Set ("Edwin M. Knowles China Co.")

Cup, 2-1/8″	5.00- 6.00
Plate, 6½″	3.00- 4.50
Saucer, 4¾″	1.00- 1.50
Teapot and Lid, 4½″	20.00-22.00

("Edwin M. Knowles China Co.")

	Dutch Figures	Floral
Cup, 2-1/8″	4.50- 5.50	3.00- 4.00
Creamer, 2-1/8″	6.00- 7.00	4.00- 5.00
Plate, 5¼″	3.50- 4.00	2.50- 3.00
Saucer, 4¾″	1.50- 2.00	.75- 1.00
Sugar, 2-1/8″	6.00- 7.00	4.00- 5.00
Teapot and Lid, 4-5/8″	20.00-22.00	14.00-16.00
Set, 4 Place	70.00-80.00	50.00-60.00

(Salem China Company)

The Little Bo Peep set on the right was called "Victory." The set on the left is marked "Godey Prints."

	Godey Prints	**Victory**
Cup	4.00- 5.00	5.00- 6.00
Creamer	6.00- 7.00	8.00- 9.00
Plate	3.00- 4.00	4.00- 6.00
Platter	6.00- 8.00	8.00- 10.00
Saucer	1.00- 1.50	2.00- 2.50
Sugar	6.00- 7.00	6.00- 8.00
Teapot and Lid	20.00-22.00	22.00- 25.00
Set, 4 Place	70.00-90.00	85.00-100.00

Basket ("Basket P.P. Salem China Co.")

Cup, 2"	4.50- 5.50
Creamer, 2¼"	6.00- 7.50
Plate, 6¼"	4.00- 5.00
Saucer, 4-5/8"	1.50- 2.00
Sugar, 2¼"	6.00- 7.50
Set, 4 Place	55.00-65.00

Waterfront Scenes

This set is unmarked, but because of shape, size and quality, we believe it to be of American origin.

Cup, 2¼"	4.00- 5.00	Sugar and Lid, 4-1/8"		5.00- 6.00
Creamer, 3 5/8"	5.00- 6.00	Teapot and Lid, 4¼"		15.00-17.00
Plate, 5¼"	3.00- 3.50	Waste Bowl		9.00-11.00
Saucer, 4¾"	1.00- 1.50	Set, 4 Place		70.00-80.00

26 Pc. Set $1⁰⁰

Beautiful Imported Blue Willow China Dinner Set

Real China!—just like the dishes Mother uses. It's hard to believe that such a wonderful 26-piece toy Dinner Set made of imported Blue Willow China can be sold at such a low price—but it's true! Note the large size pieces. Just think—it has a covered vegetable dish and a 6-in. cake plate! Each piece is traced with fine gold bands on handles and edges. The decoration is *fired-in*, will not wash off. Cups have all-over decoration. The set consists of 6 cups 2½ in. in diameter; 6 saucers 3½ in.; 6 plates 5 in.; 1 cake plate 6 in.; 1 vegetable dish 5¼ in. (with cover); 1 large tea pot (with cover); 1 sugar (with cover); and 1 creamer. Don't miss this value—it's extraordinary! Remember, this set is packed in a large *Gift Box*, about 13 by 11 in.

48 T 715—26-Piece Set. Ship. wt. 5 lbs...........$1.00

17 Pc. Set 29c

Our Lowest Priced Toy Tea Set

Really, it's quite an exceptional bargain. A beautiful China toy Tea Set with cream luster body and blue luster border with *fired-in* floral design. Contains 4 cups 2¼ in.; 4 saucers 3¼ in.; 4 plates 3¼ in.; 1 tea pot 4-in. long and 2-in. high (with cover); sugar (with cover) and creamer in proportion. In pretty *Gift Box*, about 9½ by 7½ in.
48 T 713—17-Piece Set. Ship. wt. 3 lbs..............29c

Miscellaneous China

Polka Dots

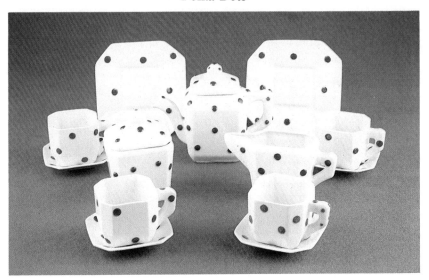

Creamer, 2½"	5.50- 6.00	Sugar and Lid, 3¾"	6.00- 7.50
Cup, 2"	3.50- 4.00	Teapot and Lid,	
Plate, 4½"	2.50- 3.50	4¼"	15.00-18.00
Saucer, 3-1/8"	1.50- 2.00	Set, 4 Place	56.00-70.00

Miniature Ironstone

Creamer	1.50- 2.00	Teapot and Lid	
Cup	1.00- 1.50	(Swan)	25.00-30.00
Plate	1.00- 1.25	Cup, 3¾"	1.50- 2.00
Sugar and Lid	2.50- 3.00	Saucer, 1½"	1.00- 1.50
Teapot and Lid	8.00-10.00	Teapot and Lid,	
Plate, Blue Onion	15.00-17.50	3-1/8"	10.00-12.00

China Miniatures

China Miniatures

Candelabrum, 3-branch, 2½"	27.00-30.00	Cup and Saucer, (Shelley)	25.00-35.00

Candelabrum,
3-branch, 2½"   27.00-30.00

Chamberstick,
(German), front
left   20.00-22.00

Chamberstick,
(Dresden), rear
left   45.00-50.00

Cheese Dish, 2½"   45.00-50.00

Chocolate Pot,
(German), 5"   65.00-75.00

Chocolate Pot,
enameled, 3"   40.00-45.00

Creamer, (Shelley)   25.00-35.00

Cup and Saucer,
(Shelley)   25.00-35.00

Dresser Set

Hair Receiver, 1¾"   27.00- 30.00

Pin Tray   17.00- 19.00

Hat Pin Holder,
2¾"   27.00- 30.00

Powder Box, 1¾"   27.00- 30.00

Set, 4 Piece   100.00-110.00

Pitcher and bowl
(Gaudy-Welsh-
type   90.00- 95.00

Food

The china food shown above is served on ironstone, glass, metal, and paper dishes. The pieces range in price from $20.00 to about $40.00. Fancy ironstone pieces are the most expensive and the paper serving pieces are the least valuable.

Children's Full-Size Dishes

Davy Crockett

Front Row: 1. Bowl, "Davy Crockett Frontiersman," 6″ $7.00-8.00. 2. Plate, "Davey Crockett," 7¼″ $4.00-5.00. 3. Bowl, "Davy Crockett," 6¼″ $7.00-8.00.
Center Row: 1. Plate, "Davy Crockett Frontiersman," 9¼″ $5.00-6.00. 2. Mug, "The Big Bear Hunter," 3-1/8″ $5.00-6.00. 3. Plate, Davy Crockett with a Bear (W.S. George), 9¼″ $5.00-6.00.
Back Row: 1. Plate, "Davy Crockett" (Royal China), 9½″ $7.00-9.00. 2. Plate, "Davy Crockett" (The Oxford China Co.), 9½″ $7.00-9.00.

Front Row: 1. Mug, "Cowboy Dog" (Knowles China Co.), 2-7/8″ $6.00-8.00.
2. Mug, "Peter Cottontail" (Homer Laughlin Co.), 3″ $22.00-25.00. 3. Hopalong
Cassidy Utensils, boxed set $24.00-26.00. 4. Hopalong Cassidy Bowl, 5-3/8″
$10.00-12.00.
Back Row: 1. Plate, "Children-at-Play" (Knowles China Co.), 6-7/8″ $10.00-12.00.
2. Baby Dish, "Jack and Jill" $8.00-10.00. 3. "Sunbonnet Babies" ABC Plate,
6¼″ $20.00-22.00.

Nursery Rhyme Scenes

Front Row: 1. Mug, "Mary Had A Little Lamb," 2-5/8″ $5.00-6.00. 2. Bowl,
"Little Bo Peep," 5¼″ $5.00-6.00.
Back Row: 1. Plate, divided, "Animals" $8.00-10.00. 2. Bowl, "Elsie," 9-1/8″
$6.00-8.00. 3. Plate, "Mary Had A Little Lamb," 7¼″ $5.00-6.00.

Front Row: 1. Bowl, "Tom, Tom, the Pipers Son," 5-3/8″ $7.00-8.00. 2. Mug, "Hickory, Dickery, Dock," 2-5/8″ $6.00-8.00. 3. Mug, "Little Boy Blue," 3″ $7.00-9.00.

Center Row: 1. Mug, "Tom, Tom, the Pipers Son," 2-5/8″ $6.00-8.00. 2. Plate, "Betsy McCall's Friends," $15.00-18.00.

Back Row: 1. Plate, "Little Jack Horner," 7¼″ $5.00-6.00. 2. Mug, "Betsy McCall's Friends" $7.00-8.00.

Plate and Mug Sets

"Children Fishing" (Noritake)

Bowl, 5-7/8″ $12.00-15.00. Mug, 2½″ $18.00-20.00. Plate, 7¼″ $10.00-13.00. Set, 3 piece $40.00-50.00.

"Barnyard Scenes" (Royal Windsor, England)

Bowl, 5-3/8″ $10.00-12.00. Mug, 3¼″ $12.00-14.00. Plate, 8″ $9.00-11.00. Set, 3 piece $30.00-35.00.

"Red Riding Hood"

Mug, 3½″ $8.00-10.00. Plate, 7″ $7.00-8.00. Set, 2 piece $15.00-18.00.

Plates, Mugs, and Bowls

Front Row: 1. Mug, "Playful Dog" (Warwick China), 2-7/8″ $12.00-14.00. 2. Mug, "Little Boy Blue," 2-5/8″ $7.00-9.00. 3. Plate, "Peter Pumpkin Eater," 7¼″ $6.00-7.00.
Center Row: 1. Bowl, "Little Miss Muffet," 5¾″ $6.00-8.00. 2. Mug, "Raggedy Ann," 2-5/8″ $4.00-5.00.
Back Row: 1. Plate, "Jack be Nimble," 7¼″ $6.00-8.00. 2. Plate, "See-Saw Margery Daw," $6.00-8.00. 3. Mug, "Ride A Cock Horse" $6.00.-7.00.

Rolling Pin

Rolling Pin, (Mary Had A Little Lamb), 9″ $55.00.-60.00.
With advertising $20.00-22.00; With no decal $15.00-18.00.

Roseville Baby Dishes

Bowl (Rabbits)	25.00-30.00
Creamer, (Rabbit)	22.00-27.00
Mug, (Rabbit)	25.00-30.00
Mug, (Dutch Girl)	60.00-65.00
Plate, (Rabbits)	20.00-22.00
Plate, (Children)	40.00-45.00

Bunnykins (Royal Doulton)

Bowl	18.00-20.00
Plate, small	18.00-20.00
Mug	18.00-20.00

The prices above are for older sets. Bunnykins is still being made. A new mug, bowl, and plate set sells for $34.95.

Dresser and Toilet Set

Pitcher, 5-3/8"; Bowl, 2-1/8"; Set $65.00-70.00

Potty, 2¼"	18.00-20.00
Soap dish, 1½" x 3½"	18.00-20.00
Toothbrush Holder,	
2" x 2½"	18.00-20.00

Wash Set ("Villeroy and Boch, Wallerfanden")

Chamber Pot, 4¼"	65.00-75.00
Slop Jar, 7-3/8"	85.00-95.00
Water Pitcher, 7¾"	85.00-95.00

Baby Reamers

Top Row: 1. $60.00-65.00. 2. $60.00-65.00. 3. $35.00-37.00.
Center Row: 1. $45.00-50.00. 2. $55.00-60.00.
Bottom Row: 1. $60.00-65.00. 2. $60.00-65.00. 3. $50.00-55.00.

Baby Reamers

Top Row: 1. $60.00-65.00. 2. $55.00-60.00. 3. $40.00-45.00.
Center Row: 1. $60.00-65.00. 2. $45.00-50.00.
Bottom Row: 1. $50.00-55.00.

PART III:
STONEWARE, METAL AND PLASTIC

Miniature Steins and Jugs

The brown earthenware steins are marked "Germany" around the top rim. The blue and white pitcher on the top row is marked "Wedgewood, Made in England." The jug on the top row, right side is Royal Doulton. The stein in the center row on the right is marked "Doulton, Lambeth, England."

Top Row: 1. (3¾") $110.00-125.00. 2. (3-3/8") $25.00-30.00. 3. (2") $35.00-40.00. 4. (2") $55.00-60.00. 5. (1-7/8") $45.00-50.00. 6. (2-3/8") $75.00-85.00.
Center Row: 1. (2¼") $35.00-40.00. 2. (1¾") $25.00-30.00. 3. (1¾") $25.00-30.00. 4. (1¾") $55.00-60.00. 5. (1¼") $45.00-50.00. 6. (2") $30.00-35.00. 7. (1-7/8") $65.00-75.00.
Bottom Row: 1. (1-5/16") $45.00-50.00. 2. (1-7/16") $45.00-50.00. 3. (1-1/8") $35.00-45.00. 4. (1-3/8") $8.00-10.00. 5. (1-7/8") $18.00-22.00. 6. (1½") $18.00-22.00. 7. (1-5/8") $12.00-14.00. 8. (1-5/8") $35.00-40.00.

Miniature Stoneware Bowls and Pie Plates

Many of the pieces shown above were used as salesman's samples. The measurements represent height. The diameters range from 2″ to 3¼″.

Top Row: 1. (1¾″) $12.00-14.00. 2. (1¾″) $12.00-18.00. 3. (1-5/8″) $35.00-45.00. 4. (1¾″) $35.00-40.00.

Center Row: 1. (¾″) $12.00-14.00. 2. (¾″) $12.00-14.00. 3. (¾″) $24.00-28.00. 4. (1″) $12.00-14.00. 5. (1¼″) $24.00-28.00. 6. (1¼″) $24.00-28.00.

Bottom Row: 1. (1½″) $45.00-55.00. 2. (1¼″) $24.00-28.00. 3. (1-1/8″) $30.00-35.00.

Miniature Stoneware

Top Row: 1. Bean Pot, 2¾″ $35.00-40.00. 2. Spittoon, 2½″ $45.00-50.00. 3. Bean Pot, 2¾″ $35.00-40.00.

Center Row: 1. Pitcher, 1-5/8″ $15.00-18.00. 2. Pitcher, 1½″ $15.00-18.00. 3. Covered Pot, "Bohemian," 2½″ $35.00-45.00. 4. Flask, 1-5/8″ $12.00-14.00. 5. Crock, "Boston Baked Beans," 1¾″ $18.00-20.00. 6. Jug, "Diamond Club Pure Rye Whiskey," 1″ with advertising $85.00-100.00. Without advertising $15.00-18.00. 7. Crock, 1-5/8″ $22.00-25.00.

Bottom Row: 1.-4. (1-1/8″) $8.00-10.00. 5.-7. Pitchers, 1½″ $14.00-16.00.

Aluminum

Bread Pan	.75-1.00	Collander	1.50-2.00
Cake Pans	.75-1.00	Measure Cup	.50-1.00
Cake Pans (Animals)	2.00-2.50	Mold, Spiral	1.00-1.50
Cannister	2.50-3.00	Muffin Tin	1.50-2.00
Casserole, covered	2.00-2.50	Pan, Fry	1.00-1.50
Coffee Pot, 2 piece	2.50-3.50	Plate	.50- .75
Coffee Pot, 3 piece	5.00-6.00	Silverware	.15- .25
Cookie Cutter	.75-1.00	Scoop	.50-1.00

Aluminum and Tinware

*Pan, 1¼″	5.00- 6.00	Funnel	8.00-10.00
*Pan, 1½″	5.00- 6.00	Funnel, 2¼″	7.00- 8.00
*Pot, 2-handle, 1½″	6.00- 7.00	Tool Set, 4 piece	42.00-45.00
*Pot, 2-handle, 2″	7.00- 8.00	Cocoa Tin	40.00-45.00
*Skillet, 1-1/8″	5.00- 6.00	*Entire set has been reproduced	

Blue Graniteware

The egg fryer pictured in the left foreground should have a handle. Add ten per cent to these prices for grey graniteware.

Casserole, covered, 2-7/8"	42.00-47.00	Ladle, 4¼"	35.00-37.00
Egg Fryer	50.00-60.00	Milk Pitcher, 2½"	45.00-50.00
Frying Pan, 4½"	30.00-35.00	Mold, Ruffled, 2¾"	32.00-35.00
Grater, 4"	50.00-60.00	Mug, 1-5/8"	20.00-22.00
		Plate, 2-3/8"	12.00-15.00

Graniteware

	Blue	Blue Band
Creamer	10.00-12.00	9.00-11.00
Cup	8.00-10.00	8.00- 9.00
Saucer	2.00- 3.00	2.00- 3.00
Sugar	10.00-12.00	9.00-11.00
Teapot and Lid	16.00-18.00	16.00-18.00
Set, 4 Place	75.00-95.00	75.00-90.00

Graniteware

The blue and white and green and white pieces at the far right are not actually graniteware, but are graniteware look-alikes.

	Bowl	Bucket	Plate
Green/White	18.00-20.00	8.00-10.00	8.00-10.00
Lt. Blue/White	20.00-22.00	10.00-12.00	9.00-11.00
Dark Blue	-------	30.00-35.00	-------
Grey	12.00-14.00	-------	-------
Cream	12.00-14.00	-------	-------
Blue/White	22.00-24.00	-------	-------
Blue/White Inside	12.00-14.00		

	Teapot	Sauce Pan
Green/White	30.00-35.00	14.00-16.00
Lt. Blue/White	32.00-37.00	16.00-18.00
Dark Blue	-------	-------
Grey	-------	-------
Cream	-------	-------
Blue/White	-------	-------
Blue/White Inside	-------	-------

	Potty	Rectangular Baker
Grey	-------	8.00-10.00
Lavender/White	40.00-50.00	-------

Copper and Brass

Top Row: 1. Copper Pans, 3 piece set $60.00-65.00. 2. Mortar and Pestle $18.00-20.00. 3. Coffee Grinder, 2″ $35.00-37.00. 4. "Daisy" Coffee Grinder, 3″ $42.00-47.00.

Center Row: 1. Teapot, 2¾″ $55.00-60.00. 2. Teapot (England), 2¼″ $45.00-50.00. 3. Teapot (Holland), 2¼″ $30.00-35.00. 4. Copper Mold, 2″ $25.00-30.00. 5. Blue and white handled silverware $8.00-10.00.

Bottom Row: 1. Utensil, 5″ $22.00-25.00. 2. Potato Masher, 3½″ 14.00-16.00. 3. Scoop, 5″ $18.00-20.00. 4. Scoop, 3″ $22.00-25.00. 5. Rolling Pin, 4¼″ $18.00-20.00.

Pewter Set

Creamer, 3¼″	22.00- 26.00	Sugar and Lid, 3½″	32.00- 36.00
Cup, 1-3/8″	16.00- 20.00	Teapot and Lid,	
Saucer, 3-5/8″	4.00- 6.00	4½″	40.00- 44.00
Spoon, 3¼″	3.00- 5.00	Set, 4 Place	220.00-250.00
Spooner, 2-5/8″	32.00- 36.00		

Pewter

Tea Set		Castor Set, 2½"	70.00-75.00
Creamer, 2-3/8"	16.00- 20.00	Castor Set, 2"	60.00-65.00
Cup, 7/8"	10.00- 12.00	Hot Water Bottle,	
Saucer, 2"	3.00- 4.00	2¼"	35.00-40.00
Sugar and Lid, 2½"	24.00- 27.00	Plate, 2-1/8"	8.00-10.00
Teapot and Lid,		Scissors, 2"	14.00-18.00
3½"	33.00- 37.00	Spoon, 1½"	3.00- 4.00
Set, 4 Place	125.00-150.00	Syrup, 4¾"	40.00-45.00
		Tray, 2¼" x 3"	16.00-18.00

Tinware

Cookie Sheet	18.00-20.00	Plate, enameled	9.00-11.00
Dust Pan	7.00- 8.00	Strainer, large	11.00-12.00
Hamburger Holder	8.00-10.00	Strainer, small	18.00-20.00
Nut Pan	35.00-37.00	Teapot	35.00-45.00
Pie Plate	3.00- 5.00	Tool Set	42.00-45.00
Plate	5.00- 6.00		

Tinware

Box	50.00- 60.00	Plate, Bicycles	60.00- 65.00
Collander	22.00- 25.00	Plate, Horse	115.00-120.00
Funnel	7.00- 8.00	Plate, Lion	110.00-120.00
Grater	20.00- 22.00	Salt Box	35.00- 37.00
Muffin Pan	8.00- 10.00	Scoops	12.00- 15.00
Pail, handled	45.00- 50.00	Seive	18.00- 22.00
Pie Tins	5.00- 8.00	Sifter	75.00- 80.00

Wagner Ware

The three pieces on the left and the small skillet in the foreground are not Wagner.

Griddle, 4½"	25.00- 27.00	Teapot (Unmarked), 2-1/8"	40.00- 45.00
*Kettle, covered, 3"	45.00- 50.00	Waffle Iron, "Freidag Mfg. Co." 4¼"	70.00- 75.00
*Kettle, open, 2½"	30.00- 35.00		
Corn Mold (Griswold, 4-1/8" x 8½"	18.00- 22.00	*Skillet, 4-3/8"	15.00- 18.00
		*Teapot, 3¾"	65.00- 75.00
Skillet (Unmarked), 3-5/8"	10.00- 12.00	*Boxed Set, 4 piece	180.00-200.00

Griswold ("Griswold, Erie, PA.")

Casserole, oval, 6″	25.00-27.00
Corn Mold, 4-1/8″ x 8½″	18.00-22.00
Kettle, covered, 4¾″	28.00-32.00
Skillet, 4-3/8″	8.00-10.00

Silverware

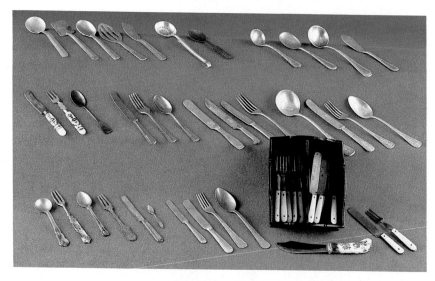

	Pewter	Bone Handle	Blue Handle	Austria/ Germany	U.S.A./ Unmarked
Silverware	1.00-1.50	8.00-9.00	8.00-9.00	1.00-1.25	.50-.75

Serving Pieces, add 50%

Little Miss Cookie Cake Decorating Set

Boxed Set   20.00-22.00

Pastry Sets

Little Busy Baker   25.00-30.00
Pastry Set No. 5902   18.00-20.00

Little Homemaker Cooking Set

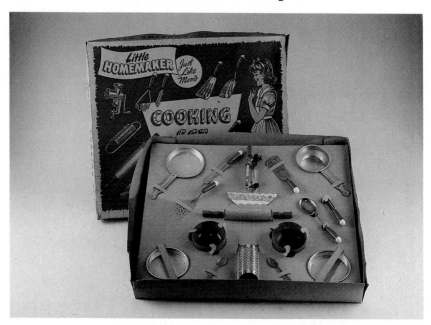

Boxed Set   18.00-20.00

Ohio Art

Little Red Riding Hood 2
  place set   20.00-25.00
Cinderella 2 place set   18.00-22.00
Mother Goose 2 place set   20.00-25.00

Fairies, 4 place set	22.00-25.00
Pinocchio, 4 place set	25.00-30.00

Ohio Art

Children, 4 place set	20.00-22.00
Rabbits and Balloons, 4 place set	22.00-24.00

Ohio Art

Little Red Riding Hood, 14
piece boxed set   20.00-22.00
Floral, 18 piece boxed set $27.00-32.00

J. Chein and Company

Strawberry, 4 place set   15.00-18.00
Candy Cane, 4 place set   15.00-18.00

Wolverine Dutch Scenes

Bread Box	10.00-12.00	Creamer	3.00- 3.50
Cake Plate	3.00- 3.50	Cup and Saucer	2.00- 2.50
Cannister, Flour	7.00- 8.00	Plate	1.00- 1.50
Cannister, Sugar	6.00- 7.00	Sugar	3.00- 3.50
Cannister, Coffee	5.00- 6.00	Teapot	12.00-14.00
Cannister, Tea	4.00- 4.50		

Wolverine

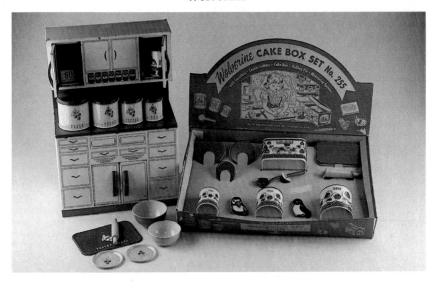

Bake Set, red and yellow, 10 pieces	25.00-27.00	Cake Box Set No. 255	30.00-35.00
Cabinet	14.00-16.00		

Alice In Wonderland

This is a celluloid set with only the sugar, creamer, and teapot bearing the "Alice" portrait.

Set, 4 Place   45.00-50.00

Ideal American Modern By Russel Wright

This little set was found advertised in a 1950's Ideal catalogue. There were three size sets available. Prices ranged from 98ᶜ to $2.98.

Boxed Set, 3 Place   25.00-30.00

172

Plastic Sets

Plastic pieces have little value except in boxed sets.

Banner Chocolate Set	13.00-15.00
"Alice" Set	12.00-14.00
Plastic Silverware, set	6.00- 8.00

It's a wonderful toy, it's IDEAL

RUSSEL WRIGHT AMERICAN MODERN TEA SET. Includes plates, cups, saucers, teapot, creamer, sugar, metalized utensils. Authentic reproduction of originals, even mottled finish . . . $2.98. Also in $1.98 and 98c. sizes.

Heavy Aluminum—Highly Polished

It includes one large 8-in. polished finish, round serving tray; 4 plates 4½ in.; 4 saucers 3¼ in.; 4 cups 2¼ in.; 4 spoons 3¼ in.; 4 paper napkins; 4 napkin rings; 1 sugar bowl 2⅛ in. in diam. and 1 creamer 2⅛ in. in diameter. Packed in attractive slotted gift box, 11 by 8 by 3⅛ inches. Ship. wt. 2 lbs.

31-Pc. Coffee Maker Set. 4-piece 6¼-in. coffee maker with wooden handle. Like full size drip pot. Makes real coffee.

48 T 948............$1.00

29-Pc. Tea Set. 2-piece teapot 5½ in. long with tea ball insert.

48 T 950..$1.00